AF620880

SEE IT TO BE IT

SEE IT TO BE IT

Eleven Champions Leading Women's Sports Today

BY BILLIE JEAN KING
WITH LIZ ROBBINS

CALKINS CREEK
AN IMPRINT OF ASTRA BOOKS FOR YOUNG READERS
New York

JACKET PHOTOGRAPHS

First row, from left: Midge Purce (Gotham FC), Caitlin Clark (Gregory Shamus / Getty Images), Amit Elor (Tony Rotundo / WrestlersAreWarriors.com). **Second row:** Diana Flores (Xinhua / Alamy), Kendall Coyne Schofield (The Professional Women's Hockey League), Asjia O'Neal (LOVB). **Third row:** Nikki Hiltz (Kevin Morris), Naomi Osaka (Clive Brunskill / Getty Images), Chelsea Gray (David Becker / Getty Images). **Fourth row:** Kelsie Whitmore (Jackie Kalafut), McKenzie Coan (McKenzie Coan / BrandonJohnsonXAR Photography).

Back flap: Billie Jean King (Billie Jean King Enterprises), Liz Robbins (Michelle V. Agins).

Text copyright © 2026 by Billie Jean King
All rights reserved. Copying or digitizing this book for storage, display, or distribution in any other medium is strictly prohibited.

For information about permission to reproduce selections from this book, please contact permissions@astrapublishinghouse.com.

Calkins Creek
An imprint of Astra Books for Young Readers,
a division of Astra Publishing House
astrapublishinghouse.com
Printed in China

ISBN: 978-1-6626-8144-8 (hc)
ISBN: 978-1-6626-8145-5 (eBook)
The Library of Congress Cataloging-in-Publication Data
is available upon request.

First edition

10 9 8 7 6 5 4 3 2 1

Design by Red Herring Design
The text is set in Rockwell.
The titles are set in Rise.

To all the young dreamers, builders,
and trailblazers—go for it!

CONTENTS

INTRODUCTION

WHEN I WAS 14, I READ THE MEMOIR OF BLACK tennis legend Althea Gibson, *I Always Wanted to Be Somebody*. I loved her story of grace and perseverance so much that I put it next to me while I slept, hoping the words would magically transfer her talent to me.

Stories will always have that power to inspire dreams. I hope this book will do the same for you.

Many of the 11 athletes you'll read about here also grew up with a book on their nightstands written by a famous female athlete. Caitlin Clark had soccer legend Mia Hamm's book. Paralympic swimmer McKenzie Coan read the memoir of Olympic gymnastics champion, Shawn Johnson. Chelsea Gray had basketball legend Cynthia Cooper's autobiography. One generation passed on wisdom to the next.

This book is coming at the perfect time because women's sports are surging in popularity. Finally! Audiences are now celebrating these athletes for their talent. New professional leagues are giving women opportunities they never had before, careers both on the field and in the franchises' front offices. Youth sports are expanding, and girls are flocking to sports like volleyball, wrestling, and flag football. Young people now have role models to guide them.

As I reflect on this era of incredible investment in women's sports and electrifying superstars showcasing their success, I can't help but look back to where it all started: the early lives of athletes.

The 11 athletes here, like so many before them, didn't just dream about being champions; they dedicated themselves to that goal from an early age. They stayed late to practice, didn't cut corners, and figured out how to balance schoolwork with sports. By the time they were teenagers competing in national and international showcases, they had already established routines that would last them a lifetime. They also had a lot of fun, fueled by their love for the sport and their achievements.

The athletes in the book make up a stacked roster of gold medalists, national champions, world champions, world No. 1s, and MVPs. They have overcome discrimination based on their gender, their race, their sexual orientation, or their disability. They dealt with doubters and dream-crushers, debilitating injuries and life-threatening surgeries. They've suffered personal tragedies. They've rebounded and won.

Along the way, some have struggled with their mental health. They shared their stories so that people of all ages can feel like they're not alone.

When I mentor young athletes, I always ask them if they're a "We" person or a "Me" person. I'm looking for people who want to pave a way, not only for themselves, but for others.

These athletes are proud members of the "We" generation. Soccer player Midge Purce started the Black Women's Player Collective and produced a streaming reality TV show about soccer. Kendall Coyne Schofield led an ice hockey players' union that worked to form a professional league. Diana Flores, a quarterback for Mexico's flag football team, advocated for Latinas in sports.

Distance runner Nikki Hiltz started an annual 5K race to support LGBTQ+ youth. Baseball player Kelsie Whitmore started a clothing brand, Be You, to inspire confidence. Tennis champion Naomi Osaka advocated for racial justice in the fateful summer of 2020, singlehandedly forcing tennis officials to halt a tournament. In her rise to the No. 1 ranking, Osaka also helped change perceptions of biracial people in her native Japan.

When I was 11, I told my mom I was going to be No. 1 in tennis. When I was 12, I decided I was going to change the world. By the time I was 17, I won my first big tennis championship—the Wimbledon Doubles title with my 18-year-old partner Karen Hantze. I missed my high school graduation for the tournament—and I don't regret it because that was the first of my 39 Grand Slam titles.

My path to No.1 began on the public courts in Long Beach, California. Here at age 12, I was practicing my backhand that would get me to the top.

Many athletes in this book missed their proms or their First Communions or sleepovers with friends in pursuit of greatness. Their dedication paid off. So did their parents' devotion. Being able to interview the moms and dads—like Elana Elor, the mother of Olympic wrestling champion Amit Elor, and Jermaine O'Neal, the NBA All-Star father of volleyball champion Asjia O'Neal—reminded me of how dedicated my own parents were in supporting my tennis dreams, especially my father. He was a true #girldad before the term became popular.

In my lifelong campaign to give girls and women equal opportunities as boys and men, I am probably most famous for my 1973 victory over a man. I defeated Bobby Riggs, a former No. 1 player in the world, with 90 million people around the world watching our so-called "Battle of the Sexes." Emma Stone played me in the 2017 *Battle of the Sexes* movie, and she made that match come back to life.

In 1974, I was proud to found the Women's Sports Foundation (WSF) in order to expand opportunities for girls and women in sports, while developing a new generation of coaches and leaders. Since the landmark 1972 law known as Title IX established that girls must have equal opportunities as boys in educational settings, we at the WSF continue to fight to protect those rights.

When people thank me for what I've done, I quickly add, "I'm not done yet!"

I still work every day. Together with my wife and business partner, Ilana Kloss, we helped form the Professional Women's Hockey League. We are also part-owners of the Los Angeles Dodgers of Major League Baseball, and with that same ownership group also have a stake in the Los Angeles Lakers of the National Basketball Association, and the Los Angeles

Sparks of the Women's National Basketball Association. We are also an owner of Angel City FC of the National Women's Soccer League.

We formed the Billie Jean King Foundation to fund organizations working at the intersection of education, activism, and sports. Then we created Billie Jean King Enterprises which supports companies for women, owned by women, such as media outlets like Just Women's Sports, The Gist, and Togethxr (which makes those iconic "Everyone Watches Women's Sports" T-shirts). We also present an award to a writer at the annual Associated Press Sports Editors conference for excellence in women's sports reporting.

In terms of media coverage, though, women's sports are still not even in the same ballpark as men's sports. In 2025, stories about women's sports amounted to only about 20 percent of sports coverage overall—another reason why I wanted to shake up the bookshelf.

You don't have to be an athlete to enjoy these words, nor do you have to identify as female. You just have to be curious about history and about what makes champions tick. For each chapter, I chose one of my favorite quotes that captures the athlete's impact.

The title of this book is the reason I wrote it, a mantra I have always repeated: "If you can see it, you can be it."

I hope seeing the journeys these remarkable young people took to become trailblazers will inspire you to write your own story.

—Billie Jean King

In sixth grade, Caitlin joined the All Iowa Attack, the top Amateur Athletic Union (AAU) basketball program for girls in the state. She led the Attack to a national championship in 2018.

CHAPTER 1

CAITLIN CLARK, BASKETBALL
"PRESSURE IS A PRIVILEGE"

ON THE FIRST DAY OF HER CLUB BASKETBALL program, 12-year-old Caitlin Clark races to the foul line, beating everyone there to accept the coach's challenge: make two free throws and no one will have to run extra sprints.

It's a big responsibility for Caitlin. She is one of the youngest of the 80 girls at the All Iowa Attack, a club known for producing high school stars.

Shaking off the pressure, Caitlin makes both free throws. The players rejoice. Caitlin raises her arms in the air.

As she walks off the court, her coach, Dickson Jensen, approaches her. "Caitlin, what are you doing?" he asks. "We've got kids here that are sophomores and juniors in high school that are top 100 players in the country. And you really think *you* should be shooting that shot? Does that make sense to you?"

Caitlin turns to him and says, "Yeah, I want to shoot it. Okay?"

Okay.

"This kid thinks she can do everything," Jensen says to himself. "Clearly at that stage, we had no idea of what that meant."

Even then, Caitlin's steely confidence was a sign of the all-around dynamo she would become: a gamer, an entertainer, and a trailblazer.

In 2024, Caitlin forever altered the sports landscape, becoming a household name and attracting legions of new fans to women's basketball. She did this first by setting the all-time scoring record in college basketball playing for the University of Iowa, where she routinely sank jaw-dropping 3-pointers from just past the half-court logo. Those shots, known as "logo 3s," became her trademark.

As the Hawkeyes' six-foot ponytailed point guard, Caitlin led Iowa to back-to-back national championship appearances. Even though her team didn't win those final games, she delivered record-breaking audiences in person and on TV.

The camera would catch her waving her arms or cupping her hand to her ear to get the crowd fired up. It was obvious: Caitlin had swagger. Kids and adults bought her No. 22 jersey in record numbers, and they lined up for autographs.

Caitlin became so popular she starred in national commercials and did a guest spot on *Saturday Night Live*. Then, after being chosen with the No. 1 pick by the Indiana Fever in the 2024 Women's National Basketball Association (WNBA) draft, Caitlin led the league in 3-point shots made and in assists. She was named WNBA Rookie of the Year in 2024.

She was following her dream. In second grade, Caitlin wrote in a class assignment that she wanted to play in the WNBA. Today, even she is surprised by the scale of her success.

“For me, I never was like, ‘I hope to be playing in front of sold-out arenas every single night.’ Or my jersey is the highest-selling jersey. Like, those aren’t things you say, like those aren’t the most important things to you,” Caitlin told me.

“That’s what happens when you put in a lot of work and just play the game the right way. All that just comes along with it, and you embrace that, and you enjoy that. But it’s all the hard work that you put in to get to that moment.”

Hard work defines every star athlete, but that’s not only what makes Caitlin Clark so special. I had the privilege of speaking to her, and I’ve watched her dazzling talent in person. I’ve been in touch with her dad, Brent Clark, and I’ve chatted with her coaches. From these conversations and from my own observations, I recognize the three qualities that turned Caitlin from a promising teen into a generational talent:

SHE'S FEARLESS. From the time she was five years old and a prodigy playing on boys’ teams, Caitlin always thought she was going to make every basket, even when she didn’t. This confidence translated off the court. As a teenager—when most girls are consumed by insecurity—she knew exactly who she was and what she wanted.

With her teammates, she’d scarf chocolate chip cookies, sing loudly at karaoke, crack jokes, and make everybody laugh. And then, when the fun was done, she’d shout out plays on the court and tell her teammates bluntly what they needed to do better.

SHE'S FAMILY-FIRST. A proud Iowa product from a large, sports-loving Catholic family in Des Moines, the state capital, Caitlin has always had a strong support network around her. They teased her, taught her respect, and molded her into the winner she is today.

SHE'S A BASKETBALL SAVANT. Caitlin always watched as many National Basketball Association (NBA), WNBA, and college basketball games as she could to memorize players' moves and recognize similar situations. She has next-level anticipation skills and incredible court vision.

"I literally think her mind and her perception ability work faster than the average person," her high school coach Kristin Meyer said.

Caitlin is like a supercomputer that can see and process mountains of data at high speed, her coaches say. She is always calculating where the other nine players are on the court, the two head coaches, the three referees, her family, friends, and even hecklers in the stands.

"I swear during a game, if someone dropped a piece of popcorn in the twelfth row, she would see it," Meyer said. "She just can take in all of her surroundings and then make decisions, knowing the speed of people, the angles."

Her college coach Lisa Bluder agreed: "She can see things before they happen."

- - - - ★ - - - -

CAITLIN ELIZABETH CLARK WAS BORN JANUARY 22, 2002, the middle child of Anne Nizzi-Clark and Brent Clark. When she started playing basketball at age five, she chose to wear the number of the day she was born.

"Honestly, I'm not a very creative person," she self-jokingly told reporters in 2024.

(I disagree that she's not creative. In numerology, the number "22" is thought to signify a person who is a "Master

Builder." I was born on November 22. Ilana, my wife, was born on March 22.)

Caitlin and her brothers are close, partly because only five years separate them. Colin is the eldest and Blake the youngest. Caitlin has many cousins—her two older female cousins played college basketball—but she formed her closest bond with six boy cousins around her age. She wanted to beat them so badly at every game.

"It's the group I wanted to run around with," Caitlin told me. "But it also didn't always turn out the best for me because they didn't take it easy on me. I would end up crying at an Easter egg hunt or whatever it was."

The boys would knock her over or block her shot with a swat. "I always was able to hold my own in some regards," she said. "But they picked on me. And whenever I would go inside crying, everybody would just be like, 'Here she goes again.' Nobody had much sympathy for me, but I appreciated that."

Caitlin could cause other people to cry, too. During a Nerf basketball game in the basement, she once shoved her brother Colin into the wall as they were both going after a loose ball. Colin needed staples.

"Obviously, I didn't take it easy on them either," she said of all the boys.

Caitlin's winning mindset was apparent even in the classroom. "I got in trouble in first grade, because I was getting so upset that I was getting second place in Rocket Math, where you get a timer and you have to complete 50 addition problems," Caitlin said, laughing. "I would go home and practice, that's just how I was."

She soon got first place.

Competition is in her DNA. Her grandfather, Bob Nizzi, was the longtime football coach at Dowling Catholic High

School in West Des Moines. Coach Nizzi once threw a tray of cupcakes in the trash at a family picnic because they had orange frosting, and orange was one of the school colors of Dowling Catholic's rival, Valley High.

Whenever Caitlin and her brothers were in the car driving by Valley, they were taught to hold their breath. They couldn't breathe the Valley air.

From her mother, Anne, Caitlin said she gets her fiery side. Brent is more analytical. "My dad, he's such a relaxed and chill guy," she explained.

It was Brent who realized Caitlin was already too advanced at age five to play basketball with girls, so he put her on the boys' team he coached for the next seven years. When Caitlin was in second grade, she led the team to a tournament victory. That caused one mother of the opposing team to complain. She didn't like seeing her son lose to a girl.

"I never thought I was different because I was playing with the boys or because I was better than most girls," Caitlin said. "I just loved to play the game. I loved to work on the game. I loved to go in the driveway and shoot baskets."

The better Caitlin became, the farther she backed up in the driveway to take longer distance shots—until she was on the lawn. So, she asked her dad to dig up part of the lawn and pave over it, giving her full 3-point range from all sides.

At times, she used other parts of the driveway to hit tennis balls against the garage, but soon she learned the tennis court wasn't for her.

Caitlin recalled one day her parents had signed her up for a group tennis lesson with kids her age. "I got kicked out of tennis class because I was upset with the instructor because it was too easy. We weren't doing actual tennis," she explained.

When Caitlin got home, her mother was furious. "My mom made me go all the way back and apologize to the instructor after the class was over, and then I never went back," Caitlin said. "But I'm sure I could have been a decent tennis player."

(This story made me so angry at that tennis coach for not challenging the kids. It also made me respect Caitlin's parents even more for teaching her good manners, as well as values that centered around their Catholic faith.)

Caitlin recalled how as a kid she worked out on virtually every holiday except Christmas. When she went to the gym on Christmas Eve, it had to be in the morning. Any later and "my mom would get mad," Caitlin said, laughing.

She never lingered in the gym, never shooting more baskets than she needed to. Her philosophy was to be efficient with her time.

From an early age, her parents never had to push her to practice or to love competition.

"Probably one of the hardest things for me to watch nowadays is that parents are so overly involved, and it's almost like it's about them more than it's about their kid," Caitlin said. "And I feel very lucky and grateful that I had two parents that just let it be my thing."

- - - - ★ - - - -

WHEN CAITLIN WAS 12, BRENT FIGURED IT WAS TIME to take her out of the local boys' basketball teams and find a challenging place where she could compete with girls her age and older. That was when she joined the Iowa Attack, a renowned Amateur Athletic Union (AAU) program 45 minutes from home, in Ames, Iowa.

Her coach and founder of the Iowa Attack, Dickson Jensen, said that Caitlin always knew how to "work the gym." She saw where the best players were warming up, and she maneuvered herself into their group. She always played on teams two grades up—until there was nowhere else for her to go but college.

For inspiration from older players, Caitlin followed her closest WNBA team, the Minnesota Lynx. In 2014, she and her dad traveled three hours to Minneapolis to see the Lynx take on the Seattle Storm. She was there for her favorite player, Minnesota forward Maya Moore, and her other favorite player, Sue Bird, the Seattle Storm star point guard.

But Caitlin wasn't wearing a Moore or Bird jersey that day. Instead, she distinctly remembers wearing a green Rebekkah Brunson T-shirt, a Lynx forward who is still the only player in the WNBA with five championship rings. (Caitlin wants to break that record.)

After the game, Moore held a Q & A session on the court for fans. "I don't even think I was supposed to be staying for that," Caitlin recalled. She and her dad made their way down by the tunnel to the floor. Then Caitlin saw her idol. "I just ran over and gave her a hug."

Caitlin didn't have a Sharpie with her for an autograph, nor did she have a phone for a selfie. The only proof she has is her memory. Caitlin went up to Moore's hip. "I felt like a little peanut next to her," Caitlin recalled.

"Even now that I'm in that position, when people just come up to you and are like, 'I'm such a big fan,' or, want to just shake your hand, or a young girl wants to give you a hug, I feel like those are the most real and authentic interactions," she said, explaining why she signs as many autographs as she can.

The dash-and-hug Caitlin had with Maya Moore was one of the rare times when Caitlin wasn't her bold self. Everywhere else she was the boss. Even on the soccer field, which competed for her time with the basketball court.

"Growing up, Mia Hamm was one of my favorite athletes," Caitlin said of the former US women's national team star forward. Hamm won four straight National Collegiate Athletic Association (NCAA) championships from 1989 to 1993 at the University of North Carolina before winning the 1999 World Cup. Caitlin had a book about Hamm that she kept on her bookshelf that she read constantly. She also had a huge North Carolina women's soccer poster in her room.

As a kid playing on club soccer teams, Caitlin had a strong shot and a creative mind. In one game when she was 11, the opposing team scored a goal, and the referee brought the ball back to the center circle so Caitlin's team could take possession. Caitlin had an idea for a totally ridiculous—but legal—play. Her coach liked it. Her teammate would pass the ball back to her and Caitlin would immediately launch a shot on goal. From about 50 yards away.

The ball sailed into the net, catching everyone off guard.

Caitlin credits the expansive soccer field for teaching her how to make long passes and how to move to open spaces on the field. As much as she loved getting an assist on a goal, she lived for scoring, especially taking a pressure-filled penalty shot.

Brent remembered one. "It was one of those deals where she just cranked it up over a whole line of defenders, over the goalie, and into the net. It was stunning," he told the *Des Moines Register*. "It was like, 'What did she just do there?' It was remarkable. Like I tell people, she's never afraid to take the last shot or the last kick. That's the best thing about it. Whether you make it or don't make it, it's the desire to take it."

Caitlin was so talented at soccer, she started as a freshman on the Dowling Catholic High School varsity team. The next year she stopped playing to concentrate on basketball.

"Quite frankly, and I'm not trying to brag about it," her dad told the local paper, "but I think she probably could have been the same sort of talent in soccer that she is in basketball."

KRISTIN MEYER WAS THE NEW GIRLS' BASKETBALL coach for Dowling Catholic when Caitlin arrived for summer workouts as an incoming freshman. That day, Caitlin threw a bounce pass three-quarters of the way down the court—about 60 feet—that seamlessly traveled between defenders and into the hands of an older teammate who converted the bucket.

Meyer was instantly struck by Caitlin's fearlessness compared to other girls on her team and around the school.

"Teenage girls, I am surrounded by them every day. And for a lot them, it's that fear that holds them back," Meyer said. "It's the fear of 'someone won't accept me,' the fear of, 'what if I make a mistake?'"

Caitlin, she said, has never been one to think: 'What if I miss the shot?' but, 'What if I make it?'"

Meyer said Caitlin was always thinking, "What if we do great things?"

Meyer brought in older boys to play in scrimmages to make it more competitive for Caitlin. (A trend that continued in college.) Her teammates were not at her talent level, which often led her to express her frustration on the court. Meyer reminded her that her attitude sometimes upset her less-talented teammates.

Other times, her teammates just marveled at her skill. During her junior year, Caitlin scored 60 points in a 90–78 victory, where she made 13 3-pointers—a state high school record. She had the couple hundred fans roaring.

"I think she plays better when she can feel that the crowd is giving her energy, and she's also entertaining them," Meyer said. "She wants to entertain people and also push her limits. She always just loved the experience, and especially if it was a big game."

When the high school basketball season ended, Caitlin went straight back to playing with her club team. It was with that team—the Iowa Attack—where she won a championship: the 2018 Nike Elite Youth Basketball League title crowning the top youth team in the nation.

That same summer after her sophomore year, Caitlin did not make the Under-17 US National Basketball team (a feeder program for the Olympic team). She called her club coach, Dickson Jensen, in tears. Caitlin wasn't upset over the injustice, but with the realization that she wasn't good enough, he recalled. "I need to be better, what do I need to do?" she asked him.

As a 15-year-old, Caitlin wasn't yet a reliably accurate shooter, Jensen said. Caitlin also hadn't grown to her current height and defenders were pushing her around. She needed the 3-pointer as her weapon.

"That was the turning point of her career," Jensen told me.

Caitlin became more disciplined about shooting, working before practice in the gym, staying late, and then using the automated ball feeder so she could get into a rhythm. Or she'd practice shooting in her driveway. Colleges took notice of her improvement.

The University of Iowa had been recruiting Caitlin since she was in seventh grade, but her parents tried to shield her from the attention and let her be a kid. They had Caitlin's older brother, Blake, get the mail before Caitlin could see any letters from college recruiters.

In high school, coaches from the University of Notre Dame and the University of Iowa were often in the stands watching Caitlin's games and practices. The one coach who didn't show? Geno Auriemma of the University of Connecticut, where Caitlin's favorite players, Maya Moore and Sue Bird, won championships. At the time, Auriemma was already recruiting guard Paige Bueckers, who would commit to UConn in the spring of her junior year. But the snub bothered Caitlin.

She was still weighing where she might carve out her own legacy. Notre Dame was an established powerhouse in the NCAA, having advanced to the semifinals or the championship game in seven of the previous nine years. Could Caitlin make a difference there? Iowa, on the other hand, had not been one of the last four teams playing in the NCAA Tournament—known as the Final Four—since 1993.

Iowa went the extra mile to recruit her. That meant not only going to watch Caitlin's high school and club games, but her international tournaments as well. Iowa's head coach, Lisa Bluder, and associate head coach, Jan Jensen, flew to Thailand in 2019 when Caitlin was playing for the Under-19 US National Basketball team.

Because of rules restricting unfair recruiting advantages, they could only watch Caitlin play—they couldn't talk to her in person. They could, however, talk to her on the phone. So Bluder, in Bangkok, gave Caitlin a call.

She could sense that Caitlin was grateful for a connection to home.

"As fearless as she is, she loves her people," Bluder said. "She loves to be around people that she really cares about. She's very family oriented."

At first, Caitlin committed to Notre Dame, arguably the most famous Catholic school in the nation. She knew that would make her parents happy.

But it didn't feel right. A few days later, Caitlin told her parents she had changed her mind and committed to Iowa. Her mom reminded Caitlin that she had to call Notre Dame coach Muffet McGraw to apologize for her turnaround.

WHEN CAITLIN GOT TO IOWA IN 2020, SHE WALKED into the locker room and noticed a small black frame hanging next to the television. Inside the frame was a note written diagonally on yellow lined paper: "To the Iowa Women's Basketball Team—Pressure is a Privilege."

Those were my words. I wrote them for Coach Bluder when I met her in 2016, and I added my signature to the note. I got to know her through my friend, Iowa's athletic director, Dr. Christine Grant (who hired Bluder). Back in 1972, Christine and I were on the front lines advocating for the passage of Title IX, the landmark law that mandated gender equity in public school settings, including sports.

> ***"No person in the United States shall, on the basis of sex, be excluded from participation in, be denied the benefits of, or be subjected to discrimination under any educational program or activity receiving Federal financial assistance."***
>
> **—Title IX, 1972**

The word "activity" might be the most important word out of that famous 37-word law, paving the way for female athletes to have the same athletic opportunities as male athletes.

I love that Caitlin walked by that frame every day of

her four-year career. Coach Bluder even read from my book, *Pressure is a Privilege*, before practices, mining it for inspiration.

"That was something that we lived by," Caitlin said. "There was always a spotlight on us, a lot of pressure to do better than we did the year before, or to perform to a certain standard. We kind of were the standard in women's college basketball."

In Caitlin's freshman season, the 2020–2021 pandemic year, crowds weren't allowed in the arena. But important people still took notice when Caitlin finished as the nation's leading scorer in Division I (DI), the highest level.

Caitlin won the 2021 Dawn Staley Award, named for the Hall of Fame point guard and current coach of the University of South Carolina women's basketball team. Dawn gets a vote as part of the committee, and the committee decides which player best displays the skills Dawn was known for in her career—ball handling, scoring, and passing.

Caitlin went on to become the first three-time winner in the award's history. "Caitlin is an absolute force," Staley said in 2023. "Someone who is quite literally changing the way basketball is being played."

Caitlin's game was about more than hitting clutch shots. Her dazzling passing skills also left teammates, opponents, and fans shaking their head in wonder. She found secret passageways through the defense, delivering perfect passes to teammates. She led the nation in assists per game for each of the last three seasons of her college career.

Against Michigan in 2024, Caitlin celebrates the moment she broke the NCAA women's all-time scoring record with—what else?—a 3-pointer near the half-court logo.

CAITLIN CKARK

"I take a lot of pride in being able to pass the ball," Caitlin told me. "I find it fun to set your teammates up and help them get a shot. It wows the crowd just as much."

The Iowa coaches embraced Caitlin's fearlessness, giving her free rein to make daring passes and take shots from anywhere. "You don't say 'Whoa!' to a racehorse," Bluder recalled.

And yet, Bluder told me, Caitlin still had to learn how to bring others with her.

During the recruiting period, Caitlin asked Bluder to recommend some books on leadership. She gave Caitlin a list, including national team soccer star Abby Wambach's bestseller *Wolfpack*, and *Lean In*, by former Facebook chief operating officer Sheryl Sandberg.

Caitlin learned to trust her teammates to catch her passes, and she worked on turning negative emotions into positive reinforcement—or at least toning down her frustrated reactions. She was still prone to outbursts, which prompted referees to whistle her for technical fouls.

Caitlin had help from one wise teammate, her best friend, Kate Martin. Some of the Iowa Hawkeyes were scared to hold Caitlin accountable, but not Kate. She was the daughter of a high school football coach, a six-foot guard who quickly gained Caitlin's respect for her similar work ethic and vision. It was Kate, not Caitlin, who was Iowa's sole captain for three straight years.

In 2023, the Iowa Hawkeyes made the Final Four for the first time in 30 years behind Caitlin's clutch shooting. The Hawkeyes then defeated the previous year's champions, South Carolina, in the semifinals to reach the title game. In that final, Iowa faced a tough Louisiana State University (LSU) team led by forward rebounding sensation, Angel Reese.

Caitlin scored 41 points, including nine 3-pointers, and dished out 12 assists. But Angel and LSU were too strong. Near the end of the game, Angel walked near Caitlin, waved her hand and then gestured to her finger. Angel was taunting Caitlin, signaling that her finger would soon be fitted for a championship ring. A rivalry was born.

But there was also an ugliness underlining the rivalry, and it had to do with race. Angel, who is Black, said she received death threats on social media from fans of Caitlin. Angel would later call out WNBA fans in Indiana for shouting racial epithets. Caitlin responded by telling reporters: "There's no place for that in our game. There's no place for that in society."

At the beginning of Caitlin's senior year, the Iowa team had become so popular, it played a preseason game in the university's football stadium. Caitlin scored 34 points and had 11 assists in front of 55,646 fans who cheered with every 3-pointer she made.

That set the tone for her senior season.

First, she became the all-time leading women's scorer in Division I, surpassing Lynette Woodard who had played for the University of Kansas in the late 1970s. Caitlin notched that first record with—what else?—a logo 3. Then she became the overall scoring leader in DI college basketball, passing Pete Maravich who played at LSU from 1967–1970. To clinch that record, Caitlin knocked down two free throws, just like she practiced as a 12-year-old at her club program. She finished with 3,951 points during her college career.

Every record and every victory seemed to bring the kind of party that Caitlin the gamer and the entertainer adored: confetti, sold-out crowds, kids in No. 22 jerseys asking for autographs, and another run to the Final Four.

This was always her favorite time of year, the final two weeks of March when 68 teams played in a high-stakes tournament, advancing round by round to win the title. Anything could happen, which is why the NCAA trademarked the basketball tournament's name: March Madness.

For a long time, though, the NCAA would only let the men's tournament use the March Madness branding on their court logos and T-shirts. That changed in 2022 after an internal investigation (prompted by a viral video from a women's college basketball player named Sedona Prince) showed the NCAA had prioritized the facilities for men's basketball, furthering gender inequity. The women could now be part of "March Madness."

Caitlin always loved the madness of both the women's and men's tournaments. She remembered sitting around on spring break with her family predicting who would win each round—penciling her selections in the tournament bracket as soon as the matchups were announced.

"I think March Madness is the greatest postseason tournament in all of sports," she said. "It's one chance, do or die. It's not a seven-game series like the NBA, or five-game series like the WNBA."

It's win or go home, exactly the type of pressure-filled challenge that fuels Caitlin.

In the 2024 Final Four, Iowa faced a rematch with Angel Reese and LSU in the national semifinal game. This time, Iowa won.

In the final, Iowa met a steamroller: Coach Dawn Staley's undefeated South Carolina Gamecocks. A total of 18.9 million people watched the competitive game on broadcast outlets, more than doubling the numbers from 2023.

Even more eye-popping? The women's championship got four million more TV viewers than the men's college championship did the next night.

Caitlin was teary-eyed in interviews after Iowa's loss. She was the consensus player of the year for the second straight year, but her team was the runner-up for the second straight time.

Her tears were about more than losing the national championship. "It was more so like, 'Dang, this ended,'" she said. "You spend so much time with your teammates, and luckily for me, my teammates were my best friends. And then, all of a sudden, in the blink of an eye and a 40-minute game, once the clock hits zero, it's over, you're not coming to practice the next day."

A week later, Caitlin was in New York City for the WNBA draft with Angel Reese and other top seniors. The players posed for glamour shots before the selections, with Caitlin wearing a specially designed white Prada miniskirt, crop top, and jacket. When the Indiana Fever chose her, as expected, for the No. 1 pick, Caitlin held up her new No. 22 jersey. Replica jerseys would soon sell out.

From the splashy draft event, it was clear the WNBA had come a long way since it began play in 1997 with eight teams and three marquee stars from the 1996 gold-medal US Olympic team: Lisa Leslie, Sheryl Swoopes, and Rebecca Lobo. Black superstars including Maya Moore, Candace Parker, and Cynthia Cooper (who led Houston to the first four titles) built the foundation of a league where approximately 70 percent of its players are Black.

Caitlin acknowledged that in an interview with *Time* magazine when she was named the Time 2024 Athlete of the Year. "I want to say I've earned every single thing, but as a white person, there is privilege," Clark told *Time*. "A lot of those players in the league that have been really good have been Black players." She added that she hoped more

Mesmerized boys and girls scrambled to get an autograph from Caitlin at the 2024 All-Star Game. Caitlin got the most fan votes, earning her a starting spot even though she was a rookie for the Indiana Fever.

"I hope that I'm making an impact in not only women's sports, with sports in general."

companies would invest in the Black players who have "made this league incredible."

With so much attention on her every word and move as a rookie, Caitlin felt pressure to perform for Indiana. And she and the Fever didn't win right away. Playing a brutal schedule against top teams, Indiana lost nine of its first 11 games. Caitlin faced larger, more physical defenders than she did in college, and they double- and triple-teamed her, forcing her into mistakes.

"I thought, why isn't it happening now? Like, you want that instant satisfaction, and so does the world," she recalled. "That's just the place we live in today. Everybody wanted me to average 30 and 10 my first night, and I didn't do that. I did the opposite."

She scored a team-high 20 points but instead of dishing out 10 assists, she turned the ball over 10 times in her debut, setting a WNBA rookie record for turnovers.

Caitlin's AAU coach, Dickson Jensen, was at one of the games in that losing streak and consoled his frustrated former star player. Jensen let her vent. And then he told her, "Okay, what can *you* do? That's it, that's all we're going to talk about for the next month."

Caitlin took on the challenge. And then she got more fuel for her frustration when she was left off the US Olympic roster of 12 players going to the 2024 Paris Summer Games.

Publicly, she said the right things about her disappointment. Privately, she told the coach of the Fever, Christie Sides, that the snub "woke a monster" in her. Sides shared that with reporters. Caitlin helped lead the Fever to six wins in their next seven games.

Caitlin was named to the 2024 WNBA All-Star team (she received the most fan votes), along with Angel Reese. Caitlin had extra motivation because her squad would face off against the WNBA players going to the Olympics in what amounted to an exhibition game preparing the US team for Paris. Caitlin had 10 assists (but just four points) and Reese had 11 rebounds, as they helped the WNBA All-Stars beat the Olympic squad.

Clark and Reese were each vying for WNBA Rookie of the Year honors until Caitlin improved dramatically in the second half of the season, leading Indiana to the playoffs. Even though the Fever lost in the first round, Caitlin earned another postseason honor: a media panel named her to the All-WNBA First Team, recognizing her as one of the top five players in the league.

Off the court, the "Caitlin Clark Effect"—what economists and the media called her economic impact—surpassed what she accomplished in college. She boosted the economic value of the Indiana Fever by more than 300 percent, brought an average of one million viewers to her broadcasted games (compared to 400,000 for the rest of the league), sold out arenas throughout the country, and contributed $36 million to Indianapolis's economy when visitors came to her games. Her jersey became the top-selling basketball jersey in the WNBA, and second among pro basketball players, behind four-time NBA champion, Steph Curry.

Caitlin understands the economics of her success. She graduated from Iowa with a degree in marketing and a minor in communications, carrying a 3.64 GPA that earned her academic all-American status.

"I hope that I'm making an impact in not only women's sports, with sports in general," Caitlin said. "And I know I am. You see it in the numbers or stats that back it up, and the people that show up to games. It's not just something that you feel or think is happening. The numbers don't lie."

Caitlin struck a familiar pose, launching a 3-pointer for the Indiana Fever just as she practiced in her driveway growing up.

In her first WNBA offseason, Caitlin lifted weights to get stronger. She worked on her shot. She also starred in a Netflix special with David Letterman where she showed off her deadpan humor and playful spirit. She filmed more commercials for her sponsors, State Farm, Gatorade, and Nike.

In what was a crossover waiting to happen, two of the most famous women in the world—Taylor Swift and Caitlin Clark—became friends. Caitlin had long been a huge Swifty, but she had also been a big fan of the Kansas City Chiefs since she was a kid. Taylor's then-boyfriend, Travis Kelce (now fiancé) was a three-time Super Bowl champion tight end for the Chiefs. Caitlin appeared in Taylor's box for a 2025 Chiefs playoff game, and of course the photo went viral.

After that joyous scene, the rest of 2025 was tough for Caitlin. When she returned for her second WNBA season, she struggled with quadriceps and groin injuries that sidelined her. She played in just 13 games of the 44-game season. As she wrote in a social media post in September 2025 announcing that she would not return from injuries, "disappointed isn't a big enough word to describe how I am feeling."

It was the longest Caitlin had been out of action in her career, but she was determined to get healthy for her future. Already, she had been contemplating her post-playing career.

Caitlin was part of an owners' committee bidding to bring a National Women's Soccer League (NWSL) expansion team to Cincinnati. (Their bid wasn't selected.) At the time, soccer was just a placeholder for her sports business dreams.

"I wish I could own part of a WNBA team," she told me, and then laughed. "That's illegal, so once I'm done playing, that's my goal."

Like she does on the court, Caitlin is visualizing several moves ahead. She observes how women's professional franchises are skyrocketing in value, with the expansion Golden State Valkyries hitting $500 million in 2025. Angel City FC in the NWSL sold for $250 million in 2024.

"It's very evident where sports are going," Caitlin said. "Who wouldn't want to be an owner of a women's sports organization right now?"

Especially if that organization has her.

Can't Touch Me: Diana, 14, evaded a defender in a youth flag game in Mexico. As a teenager, she also gained experience playing for a suburban Philadelphia club in the summer.

CHAPTER 2

DIANA FLORES, FLAG FOOTBALL

"YOU HAVE TO SEE IT TO BE IT"

DIANA FLORES DASHES ACROSS THE PARKING LOT, her sleek black ponytail flying behind her, yellow flags on her belt shooting like flames from her waist.

She zigs. She zags. She spins and sprints ahead. The men and women trying to pull her flags fall flat on the ground.

CUT!

Flores, a five-foot-two quarterback for Mexico's women's flag football team, is filming a television commercial for the 2023 Super Bowl, and I was there to make a cameo appearance. Little did we know our time together that day would lead to a lasting friendship.

Let me set the stage. The National Football League (NFL) wanted to promote the rapid growth of flag football, a sport where, instead of tackling players to the ground, the defensive team tries to grab a flag from a belt at the ball carrier's waist to end the play. Flag football has more than

2.4 million kids under 17 playing in the United States, and the NFL is its largest organizer.

Diana was a natural to play the leading role in the commercial. She had hurdled difficult obstacles as a kid—from having to clear trash off the girls' field in Mexico City to convincing coaches a small girl could play quarterback—before leading Mexico to the 2022 World Games championship and then winning the title again in 2025.

I always look out for the next generation of athletes, and I do my best to ensure that they succeed. That day on the set of the commercial, I was there to act it out. The director put me in the driver's seat of an SUV in the parking lot of SoFi Stadium in Inglewood, California.

ACTION!

I opened my car door to block the path of a parking enforcement officer just as he came running after Diana.

"Oops!" I said, grinning while looking down beneath my red-rimmed glasses at the stunt actor.

In the commercial, as in real life, I would do anything to protect the future of women's sports. Diana is part of that future.

You know when you can instantly tell somebody is special? It's in the way they smile, look at you, hold their back straight and project confidence but not arrogance. The way they are curious and engaged in listening to everything you're saying. That's Diana.

We had a chance to talk in her trailer while on a shooting break. I didn't waste time. "What do you want to do now?" I asked.

"I want to make a change," she said.

We talked some more, and then I asked, "What do you really want to do?"

"I want to make a change," she answered again.

I loved that she never wavered. "That passion, that joy you answered me with—you're going to need these," I told her. "Because making a change is not easy. Making a change will take you time. A lot of time. Making a change will take strength from you."

Diana understood. Her grand ambition to empower girls to become leaders on and off the field was bigger than her personal aspirations. Our meeting would spark late-night texts and chats between us, two athletes from different eras who had faced discrimination but would not be denied. Of course we want to win, but we also want the same thing for women in sports: more opportunities, more teams, more athletes, more money, more recognition.

Flag football is in its infancy compared to other sports for girls, but it is growing rapidly in high schools in the United States. In the 2024–25 school year, 68,847 girls played on their high school teams, a 60 percent increase from the previous year. Flag football will debut in 2028 as an Olympic sport for men and women at the Los Angeles games. Diana plans to be there to win a medal.

DIANA WAS BORN IN 1997 IN MEXICO CITY, THE oldest of three children to Jaime and Josefina Flores. She spent hours playing tag in her family's backyard with her brother and sister. When they outgrew their home's brick-walled garden in the Santo Tomás neighborhood, they took to the street where there were no rules and no out of bounds. No one could catch Diana there, either.

By the time Diana was eight, her father introduced a new game, one that added a ball. Unlike most kids who kicked a

Jaime Flores, Diana's dad, introduced her to the sport in their hometown of Mexico City when she was eight years old. She's been winning trophies ever since.

round ball in Mexico City—*fútbol* in Spanish—Diana was running with an oblong one. An American football.

Jaime Flores had learned to play football at age ten when a boy in his neighborhood showed him the game. They'd play a version in the street without tackling—touch football or *tochito*—and he loved it so much, he graduated to the tackle kind as a teenager.

As a young parent, Jaime heard there was a new football program for girls in which opponents would try to rip *banderas*, or flags, hanging from a belt of a ball carrier. This seemed a more competitive version of *tochito*, and Jaime was excited to teach Diana how to throw a perfect spiral.

Diana used a smaller football because her hands were still quite small. Amazingly, it only took her four tries to master throwing a perfect spiral. She was ready. She just needed to find a team.

At the time, girls played flag football in Mexico, but they were at least five years older than Diana. Jaime signed her up for the team, but he couldn't convince Coach Julio César Ocaña—who used to be one of Mexico's best tackle football players—to let her onto the field. Ocaña was concerned that she was too tiny. Eventually, Diana convinced him with her grit and her blinding speed. He put her at receiver, but he still wouldn't let her play quarterback.

Just getting on the field was a major accomplishment for Diana and her team. This program separated the boys and the girls. The boys played on the nicer field. The girls? They had to clear trash and rocks from an adjacent dusty field each day before practice. Diana didn't know any better. If that's what she had to do to play, she would pick up trash.

Flag football was just one of Diana's many after-school activities, along with piano, gymnastics, karate, and ballet.

Her sister, Montserrat, who is six years younger than Diana, would become a talented pianist.

"We are all very competitive, but she's next level," her younger brother Jaime said of Diana. "Everything she does, she needs to be at the top. It's not only a mindset, she actually does it."

Her father told me she was the type of child who would insist on coloring precisely inside the lines. If she messed up, it would be "a whole drama," Jaime said. The drawing had to be perfect. Her brother, five years younger, agreed. She was his coach.

"Everything I learned, I learned from her," her brother Jaime said. "I practiced . . . with her. The agility moves, the cuts, how you run the routes. She taught me how to throw the ball. I learned more from Diana than I did from my coaches."

He added: "With her, it's always perfection. It was not just about a perfect ball, it needed to be the perfect placement, the perfect timing, the perfect moment."

Here's the beautiful thing—neither her father nor mother put pressure on her to be perfect. Diana was the one who was hardest on herself. "Instead of my parents telling me to focus more or to do things well," she said, "they were telling me the opposite—'it doesn't matter, it's about having fun.'"

They also taught her to be respectful to her elders and to honor their Catholic traditions. When it came time for Diana's First Communion, marking her first step toward adulthood in the community, her participation was nonnegotiable.

The problem was, on that same Sunday, Diana's team was playing a championship flag football game on the other side of the city. Her teammates were five years older, so they had already made their First Communions. Diana pleaded with her parents to skip the ceremony, to no avail.

Diana's mom, Josefina, wanted to put Diana's hair up in a bun for the ceremony. Diana refused because it would mess up the cute ponytail she wore during games. Her mother compromised with a loose updo. Her parents also agreed to forgo the traditional party after the First Communion Mass so they could get to the game.

Diana made a concession, too. She would wear her fancy white dress, but only if she could wear her black spandex shorts under it. The moment the ceremony ended, Diana ducked into the church bathroom, took off her dress, handed it to her mother, and said, "Let's go!"

Her team won the championship. A double celebration for Diana.

DIANA DECIDED AT AGE 13 THAT SHE WOULD concentrate on "flag," as the players call it, and phase out her other activities. She would still use the graceful dance moves she learned from ballet and show off her uncanny balance when escaping defenders trying to snatch away her flags.

Because of her age and size, people still underestimated her. The older girls resented her because she was trying to take the prized position of quarterback. If only Diana had a role model to follow.

Instead, she turned to the internet to find an athlete she could relate to, someone who changed people's views on female athletes. That's when she came across a historic international event: "Billie Jean King Beats Bobby Riggs in the 1973 'Battle of the Sexes.'" She figured if Billie Jean King could do it at a time when few people believed in female athletes, then so could she.

Her biggest supporters were her family, and that explains the origin of her uniform number. She originally wanted to wear No. 3, to honor the number of siblings in her family. ("So, I could feel like they were always with me!" she said.) But No. 3 was taken. She doubled it.

By then, Diana was traveling with her Mexican club team to tournaments in the US. In 2010, she was in Boston where she met a girls' team from Philadelphia coached by Mike and Matt Reimel. Their youngest brother, Jeff Reimel, was a couple of years older than Diana and played on the boys' team the brothers also coached.

Jeff kept in touch with her via direct message on social media—Facebook Messenger at the time. When they talked on Skype, his older brothers Mike and Matt got on the screen to talk flag football. All three convinced Diana to join their girls' team outside Philadelphia—North Penn (NP) Flag—for a few tournaments.

The first one was in 2012, when Diana played receiver. NP Flag then was invited to a national tournament in New Orleans the week before the 2013 Super Bowl. The Reimel family took Diana with them.

Three months later, Diana's parents returned the hospitality, hosting Jeff and Mike in Mexico City. At the end of their visit, Jaime and Josefina felt comfortable sending their daughter back to Philadelphia with the Reimels for a summer of flag football. For the next five summers, Diana stayed in the Reimel's modest split-level house in Lansdale, Pennsylvania—a suburb 15 miles northwest of Philadelphia—with parents Tracy and Kevin Reimel. Mike and Jeff's sister, Kitty, who was home from college, was also in the house. Matt, who now runs NFL FLAG football tournaments, had moved out so there was room for one more. Diana, said Mike, became the "fifth sibling."

She helped NP Flag win a regional NFL-sponsored championship that first summer. Mike was amazed by Diana's accuracy passing the ball, her speed, and her agility. In flag football, the ability to change direction quickly is known as "hip skills," and Diana could move her hips almost like she was dancing. When opponents lunged for a flag attached to her belt, she had already pivoted and was headed up field with the ball.

"Everything I've asked her to do, she's done on the football field. Off the football field, as far as training, there's no hesitation," Mike said. "She's a 'yes person.' She just wants to be better."

Diana begged her parents to let her stay in Philadelphia for high school. She was nearly fluent in English, and she already knew girls who went to North Penn High School. They said no. In retrospect, Mike said, it was the smartest decision for Diana's career. At the time, there were only about 10 travel flag football girls' teams in the Northeast, so she wouldn't have had much competition. In Mexico, the sport had progressed to where girls could play throughout the year and then compete in college.

When Diana returned from Philadelphia that first summer, she was approaching another rite of passage in Latin American culture—the quinceañera, which celebrates a girl becoming a young woman at 15. Diana had no interest in wearing a fancy, flouncy dress to mark the milestone. Her idea of a party was playing flag football.

By the time she was 15 years old, Diana was a key player for the Mexican junior national team, which had an important tournament in Le Havre, France, around her birthday. At this point, her parents knew they couldn't win the argument. Instead of throwing Diana a party, they funded the trip as a quinceañera present.

It was clear that Diana was not one to stick to traditional gender roles. That upset some of her conservative teachers at Instituto Politécnico Nacional in Mexico, a high school focused on science, technology, engineering, and math (STEM). Diana was one of three girls in a class of 40. She studied STEM, with a concentration in robotics, all while competing in flag football. That meant she often would miss class for a few days, sometimes even a week, for tournaments.

When she returned, there was one teacher who did not appreciate her absence. "She wouldn't even let me go into her class," Diana said. "Literally, she would close the door in front of my face and let my classmates go in." The teacher would not even tell Diana the material that had been covered in class. Diana had to get the lesson from her friends.

"My parents were like, 'You're going to ask your classmates and you're going to study by yourself, and you're going to be the best at that subject, and you're going to pass all the tests,'" Diana recalled.

Some of Diana's male teachers weren't any kinder. They would make fun of her when she wore her favorite skirts because her bare legs revealed bruises from the past weekend's game. They looked at her disapprovingly. "How are you going to get a husband?" one teacher said.

The treatment got even worse when she'd return to class limping. "How are you going to have babies?" another male teacher said to her.

When Diana would get an A, one teacher demanded, "Who helped you with this?" Another told her that she shouldn't even be studying math since boys were naturally better at it.

Her father witnessed all the discrimination, from the rocks on the girls' field to the dismissive comments from her teachers. He chose to boost his daughter's spirits, rather than complain and make things worse for her.

"As a father," Jaime said, "I would see all these things, but I also told her, 'You are powerful, you can do this.'"

Diana did her homework and concentrated on flag, doing her best to tune out the negativity. It wasn't easy. The loudest voice was her own, and today she admits that she wasn't always nice to herself as a teenager.

"I was upset, exhausted, almost like having to fight against what people think all the time, rather than just showing what you can do," Diana recalled.

At times, the pressure to succeed in the classroom and on the field became overwhelming for her mental health. She'd curl up in a ball in bed and tell her parents she wanted to skip practice or skip school.

"A grade doesn't define who you are, a loss doesn't define who you are," her parents would say. "It does depend on your attitude you had that day, on the effort you put, and the learning you got from that. So it doesn't matter if you lose, if learn from that, if you enjoyed the moment, if you had fun, you're winning."

When she debated whether to quit, her parents again gave her the power to choose. "If you quit, it's because you decided, not because people tell you to give up," they told her.

Diana decided to keep playing, enrolling at the prestigious Tecnológico de Monterrey university in Santa Fe, Mexico, home to one of the top women's flag football teams in the country. Playing quarterback, she won three national titles for the Borregos (the Rams) and finished with both undergraduate and graduate degrees in marketing and communications.

In 2021, Diana finally was named the starting quarterback for the Mexican national team at the World Championships;

she was also named the team captain. Although Mexico lost to the United States by 10 points, Diana was already calculating what she could do better.

At the 2022 World Games in Birmingham, Alabama, 25-year-old Diana quarterbacked her team to the gold medal. Mexico trounced the US team, 39–6. Mike and Matt Reimel were there to support her. When they went down to the field after the game, waiting out the crowd of well-wishers, Diana rushed over to give them a hug. "I wouldn't be here today if it wasn't for you guys," she said softly.

From there, Diana's success accelerated. Under Armour, the sports apparel company, signed her to an endorsement contract. She was named to the athletes' committee for the International Federation of American Football, the body that oversees flag football.

Diana became an NFL ambassador to help publicize the sport. In 2023, the league invited her to the NFL Pro Bowl, the league's all-star game, where the best players faced off in a game of flag football, the noncontact competition ensuring fewer injuries. Diana was named offensive coordinator for one of the teams and got to call plays with legendary NFL quarterback Peyton Manning, who was the coach.

That Pro Bowl experience was a turning point in her career, she said, because it helped her appreciate the value of mentorships, and how to collaborate with others to boost opportunities for women in the sport. Since then, she has worked Super Bowls in the broadcast booth as a commentator for Spanish language television, putting her communications degrees to good use.

"Diana was born with an incredible gift," said Sam Rapoport, a former NFL executive who grew up playing flag football in Canada. Rapoport is impressed with Diana's communication skills as much as her enthusiasm to promote flag football.

"When I speak to her about the landscape of flag football in this country, in the world . . . she's very passionate about girls' and women's rights and doing things the right way to ensure that girls and women are leading in this sport," Rapoport said.

Rapoport led the effort to create NFL-sponsored youth flag football leagues (for boys and girls) that operate in addition to high school teams, like the club system in basketball or soccer. The NFL took note of the rapid growth of youth leagues, and in October 2025 announced that it was "committed" to starting men's and women's pro leagues "in the next couple of years."

Rapoport credits other trailblazers beyond Diana, especially US quarterback Vanita Krouch, who was born in 1980 in a refugee camp for Cambodians in the Philippines and grew up in the US. Krouch has led the US women's team in international competitions for two decades.

The final scene of Diana's Super Bowl commercial sponsored by the NFL shows her running down a suburban street, flanked by other female players, including Krouch. The end title reads: "To the women pushing football forward, we can't wait to see where you take this game."

Based on statistics and stories, there's no question that the 2023 NFL commercial helped bring new players to the sport. Before the commercial? In the 2022–23 season, 20,875 girls played high school flag football, according to high school federation statistics. After, in the 2023–24 high school season, 15 states sanctioned girls flag football, with a total of 42,955 girls playing. The numbers had doubled and didn't stop there. At the end of the

2024-2025 high school year, a 1,000 more schools across the United States offered flag football for girls, with a total of 68,847 players.

The impact of trailblazers like Diana goes beyond numbers, however. In 2023, Mike Reimel was coaching a girls' high school team in Philadelphia, and Diana graciously FaceTimed with them to wish them luck before a big game. A senior on his team asked to speak to Diana in Spanish to ask for advice. She was of Mexican heritage, and her own father encouraged her to play, just like Diana's dad.

"I'm playing because of her commercial," the girl later told Reimel.

Mike now runs a business dedicated to flag football tournaments. To satisfy the demand for girls in the sport, he created a girls' flag tournament tour called "We Run the World," after the Beyoncé song.

In October 2023, Diana made an appearance at that tournament, held at AT&T Stadium, home of the Dallas Cowboys. Nearly five hundred girls of all ages represented 188 teams. When Diana headed down to watch the action on the field, clusters of girls crowded around her for autographs and selfies. She then asked the girls what position they played, thanked them for playing, and even signed seven footballs for one mom.

Mike told Diana that he would control the crowds for her if she wanted. "I'm your big brother." he said. "I got you."

Diana shook her head. "No, Mike," she said. "I didn't have anyone to look up to in flag football, and I want to be that person for these girls. I didn't choose to be it, but I'm not going to let them down."

Diana subscribes to one of my core values: to succeed young people need an example of someone who comes from a similar background or who had similar experiences. She knows what I know:

"YOU HAVE TO SEE IT TO BE IT."

AT THE 2025 WORLD GAMES IN CHENGDU, CHINA, eight women's flag football teams competed for the championship, playing five players to a side. As expected, the United States and Mexico faced off—in a rematch of the 2022 World Games—for the title. The game came down to the thrilling final seconds.

All tournament, Diana led her teammates in a chant of their singular goal: *¡Piensa En Oro!* Think of Gold!

With 28 seconds remaining, Mexico was trailing the United States flag team, 21–20. Vanita Krouch, the 45-year-old US quarterback had just led her team on what seemed like a game-winning touchdown drive. But Diana and Mexico took advantage of the US team's mistakes in that final half-minute. The Mexican players found themselves close to the end zone for one final play. Three seconds remained on the clock.

At quarterback, Diana took the snap, scanned the field, and saw that receiver Victoria Chávez was all alone in the end zone. Diana calmly threw the perfect pass, and Mexico rejoiced.

In an on-field interview posted on her Instagram page, Diana shouted jubilantly in Spanish: "*¡Somos Oro!*"

"We are Gold!"

The closeness of Mexico's victory compared to the 39–6 drubbing of Team USA in 2022 showed how the level of play had risen in three years. "It has been amazing to be part of that movement, to be part of that change and alongside my team kind of like push the sport forward. I think competitiveness is essential for the growth of the game," Diana said after the 2025 championship on the podcast, *Good Game with Sarah Spain*.

- - - - ★ - - - - -

I OFTEN THINK BACK TO WHEN WE WERE FILMING the commercial for the NFL. Few people outside the flag football community knew who Diana was. Even she didn't realize she was going to be the star of the commercial.

When I met Diana at the next day of the commercial's filming, I had a request. I brought one of the yellow flags that players wear on their belts. I asked her about the one word that drives her, the word that motivates her when she's feeling down, and I told her to write that on the flag. She wrote, "Inspire."

Every story I hear about Diana tells me she is continuing to do that.

Today, Diana runs her own camps for young girls in Mexico through her sponsor, Under Armour. She told me a story from a camp in 2023 that has stayed with her. Diana had a Moroccan friend who asked her to participate in a camp for underserved young girls in Rabat, Morocco, to bring the sport to a new country.

For many of the girls, age 10 to 19, this was their first time playing flag football. For others, it was also their first time playing sports. Some girls were wearing hijabs, the traditional headscarf covering for Muslim women.

For two hours a day during the four-day camp, Diana taught skills and ran drills, while her friend translated in Arabic. She remembers how one 10-year-old was so shy, she did not talk to anyone or make eye contact on the first day.

Diana quarterbacks Team Mexico past host China in the quarterfinals of The World Games in 2025.

"I didn't have anyone to look up to in football, and I want to be that person for these girls."

Diana threw five touchdowns against Japan in the opener of the 2025 World Games. Three days later, she lifted Mexico to a last-second victory over the United States to capture the championship.

Gradually, the girl joined in, wearing a pair of ragged sneakers too small for her feet. By the last day when the teams played a full game, the girl was laughing.

Diana pulled her aside. She gave the girl her own cleats—size 6.5, they fit her perfectly—and told her how brave she was for coming to the clinic: "I want to give you these, because I know that a bright future is a waiting for you, and I know you're going to do great things."

The 10-year-old was wide-eyed and thankful. And when she returned to her new friends, cleats in hand, she burst into tears.

Diana panicked. Had she made a mistake with the shoes? Had she said something wrong? She asked the older girls.

They explained, "She was emotional because it was the first time someone had told her she had a bright future, not even her parents had said this."

Diana will never forget this moment. It inspires her today. "I want little girls to know that they belong," she said, "that they belong to this field."

Kendall continued playing for the boys' Chicago Chill hockey team in 2003, even though it was an hour away from her house.

CHAPTER 3

KENDALL COYNE SCHOFIELD, ICE HOCKEY

"ASK FOR WHAT YOU WANT AND WHAT YOU NEED"

KENDALL COYNE BURST INTO A BLUR. SKATING FROM goal line to blue line to red line and back again, she went all out, never coasting during the last few strides as some boys were doing. When the whistle blew, she came to a two-foot stop, her blades spraying the ice like an exclamation point.

Coach Larry Pedrie of the Chicago Chill had come to expect such maximum effort from Kendall. He chose her to be on his boys' ice hockey team as a nine-year-old, even though she was the youngest and smallest. He knew her speed would create scoring chances for teammates, and her hustle would make everyone around her better.

Coach Pedrie was right. He was right about something else, too.

"One day," Coach Pedrie told the boys on that team, "You're all going to be buying tickets to watch Kendall."

In 2024 and 2025, a total of 17,333 fans bought tickets to watch Kendall captain her Minnesota team to back-to-back championships in the first two years of the Professional Women's Hockey League (PWHL). It was a league she helped create.

"Women's hockey is here, it's here to stay," Kendall said. "You can feel and see the significance of what it means, not only to sports, but society."

Kendall became a trailblazer in a traditionally male-dominated sport because she chased after her dream like she was sprinting after a loose puck. She got there first and made something happen.

She also had my help. This is where Kendall's story intersects with mine, generations apart, in a sport I didn't follow much until I met her in 2019.

At the time, Kendall was totally fed up with the lack of opportunities and low pay women hockey players had to accept to be professional athletes. Kendall needed advice. She called her friend and mentor, Angela Ruggiero, the youngest member of the 1998 gold medal-winning Olympic women's hockey team and a four-time Olympic medalist.

Angela, who had served as president of the Women's Sports Foundation, which I founded, told Kendall she had to speak to the two people who could make a difference: "You have to call Billie Jean and Ilana," she said.

Angela connected her with me and my wife, Ilana, who is the chief executive of Billie Jean King Enterprises, our women-owned consulting and investing firm. I always like to say, "I dream it, and Ilana builds it." In this case, Kendall was sharing her dream with us, asking us to help build it.

When Kendall, all of five-foot-two, walked into our home with a notebook to tell us the grim realities of working three jobs just to afford to play hockey, she convinced us to explore ways to make a league work.

I always tell elite athletes: "Ask for what you want and what you need." That's what I did when I secured a $55,000 sponsorship from Bristol Myers (and their Ban deodorant) that enabled the United States Open to pay women tennis professionals the same prize money as men in 1973.

"I think what we've learned so often is you can ask, but we're oftentimes met with resistance," Kendall said. "We're met with excuses. We're met with discrepancy, inequity."

Kendall wanted to add something to my motto: "Ask for what you want, but be prepared to *fight* for what you need," she told me. "Or what you deserve."

Ever since Kendall came to me and Ilana, I have been amazed by her singular drive. She's so focused on making this young league work, while making her own game great and her teammates better. And then, as if she didn't have enough on her plate, in 2024, the first year of the PWHL, she and her husband, Michael Schofield, were also busy raising their infant son, Drew.

In getting to know her, I can see how Kendall's own Chicago family molded her and encouraged her to succeed. They are a big part of her story, how she transformed from a small girl in hockey skates to a driven teen playing for junior national teams to a trailblazer lifting a championship trophy and winning gold medals.

KENDALL WAS BORN IN 1992, THE SECOND CHILD OF John and Ahlise Coyne. Her brother, Kevin, was nearly three years older, and both were extremely active children in their town of Palos Heights, a suburb southwest of Chicago. Her father John, an attorney for the state of Illinois, was an avid baseball player. Ahlise, a teller at a bank and a racetrack, had been a tumbler in gymnastics and a softball player. All four of their children would play ice hockey.

Baseball proved too boring for Kevin. As a five-year-old standing in the outfield, he had trouble seeing the long fly balls coming toward him. He needed a sport with more up-close action. Kendall was going to follow him, no matter what.

Luckily for the energy-infused Coyne siblings, a new suburban Chicago rink was offering free after-school hockey and skating lessons. When Kevin went with the boys, Kendall reluctantly went to the girls' side of the rink to try figure skating. That lasted just two lessons before she begged her parents to let her wear hockey skates and play with the boys.

Kendall soon loved to go fast, and, gradually, she figured out how to control her speed. She also had to control her long blond hair when it flew outside her helmet and blocked her vision. That inspired the ritual of her mom braiding her hair before practice. But if Ahlise had to work while the kids were at the rink, a young Kevin took over braiding his sister's hair. He would do anything for Kendall, and vice versa.

She loved the game and soon was advancing faster than the boys on her team. When Kendall tried out for an advanced travel club for seven-year-olds, however, the coach told her father devastating news: "I don't think she'll ever be travel hockey material."

When John pressed him to explain why, the coach made

excuses. The truth was clear. The coach didn't select her because Kendall was a *girl*.

All Kendall wanted to do was play hockey; she would keep practicing to convince the next coach that she belonged.

"It forced me to be a good skater because I knew I never wanted to lose the opportunity to play this game," she said.

Many elite athletes can trace their love for the sport from the time spent practicing it with their siblings in the backyard or in the driveway. In the case of the Coyne family, practice was in the basement.

Ahlise Coyne painted the cement floor ice blue to resemble a rink but kept the walls unfinished. Today, those concrete walls bear thousands of black puck marks, each one a shot from an imaginary Olympic gold-medal game, or a real Coyne victory.

Kevin and Kendall have two younger siblings: Jake, three years younger than Kendall, and Bailey, four years younger. All four Coyne children played hockey competitively, but because they were closest in age and size, Kendall and Kevin had the fiercest battles.

Usually, one of them would hit the other with a stick or shove each other into the wall. They played with an NHL-regulation hockey net—which the family bought for a Canadian dollar discount in Toronto and then drove it back across the border. They'd wear socks or Rollerblades, shouting and scraping. Ahlise encouraged the activity and embraced what she now jokes as the "dysfunction" of her family. It certainly worked for them.

Ahlise found a club an hour away from their home that would take both Kevin and Kendall. That was the Chicago Chill and Coach Pedrie's team.

"It was an easy decision," Pedrie said about putting

Kendall on the team. "She had a motor from day one and never stopped working."

The boys treated Kendall as an equal, in part because Coach Pedrie taught them to do so.

"I was just another hockey player on the ice with them," she recalled. "I happened to be the only girl surrounded by a bunch of boys. A lot of them were really good to me. But I also think it taught me to believe in myself. It is hard to walk into a room when you don't look like anybody else, and to be confident right away."

Sometimes when her team went to other rinks, she could hear nasty comments from parents of opposing team members who were worried about Kendall showing up their sons.

"You don't belong here!" the parents shouted.

"Get off the ice!" they added.

Kendall figured the adults were yelling at her because they were bothered by her challenging the status quo.

Kendall (No. 7 front row, third from right), was the youngest and smallest on the 2002 Chicago Chill AAA Boys Hockey Team. Her coach, Larry Pedrie, didn't think twice about choosing her. "She had a motor from day one and never stopped working," he said.

"Just because it's been done this way for as long as some people can remember, doesn't mean that's the way that it should always be done and can be done," she said.

FOR SO LONG, IT SEEMED THAT THE ICE WAS ALWAYS reserved for male hockey players. The sport was part of the first Winter Olympics in 1924, but women's hockey players were not even allowed to play in the Olympics until 1998.

On the off years between the Olympics, the International Ice Hockey Federation held a world championship tournament for men starting in 1930. The women's world championships did not start until 1990.

In 1992, Quebec-born goalie Manon Rhéaume became the first woman to play in a National Hockey League (NHL) game when she suited up in an exhibition game with the Tampa Bay Lightning. But she never made it into the big leagues for a regular season game.

The sport took a big leap forward when women's ice hockey debuted at the Winter Olympic Games in Nagano, Japan. The US team, which had spent months together training in Lake Placid, New York, triumphed 3–1 over rival Canada in the gold-medal game.

Kendall, who was six at the time, didn't get to see it live because of the 13-hour time difference, but she knew all about it. A few months later, her parents took her to a hockey camp run by the US Olympic team captain, Cammi Granato. At the camp, Granato let Kendall hold her gold medal, and from that moment, Kendall was determined to win her own. She hung a poster of Granato next to the bunk bed she shared with her younger sister, Bailey.

Those Olympics did not boost professional opportunities

in the United States. But a women's league formed in Canada to start the 1998–99 season, called the National Women's Hockey League (NWHL). That league would eventually fold, but several different professional women's hockey league attempts were made in the years to come.

As an 11-year-old in Chicago, Kendall was selected to a North American all-star team that was the first girls' squad to compete in a premier youth tournament for boys in Québec. Rhéaume, the first woman to suit up in the NHL, coached Kendall's team and convinced officials to include the girls' team.

In the opening game, Rhéaume recalled that some fans shouted at the girls in French: "*Retournez à la cuisine!*"—"Get back in the kitchen." How original.

Kendall remembered that others threw hot pennies onto the ice by the girls' bench, which melted the surface and were meant to mess up the players' blades. Kendall knew just how to quiet them. She scored goals.

The girls advanced to the semifinals of the tournament and even earned airtime on ESPN. But the organizers did not invite them back the next year in order to avoid controversy.

Because she knew how gifted Kendall was, Rhéaume invited her to play on another all-girls team in nearby Wisconsin. Kendall's team won the state tournament that year. The next year when Kendall aged out, she joined a team in Michigan, again based on Rhéaume's recommendation. But when Kendall, then barely five-feet tall, showed up the first day hauling an equipment bag bigger than she was, the male coach was visibly disappointed.

At least until he saw her beat everyone to the puck.

"OK, I'm good," the coach said, turning to Rhéaume and smiling.

While Kendall also enjoyed playing softball, by the time

she was a junior in high school, she was specializing in hockey. As she played in tournaments all over the Midwest, that meant thousands of miles of driving for her mom, Ahlise.

They'd stay in hotel rooms together, but Ahlise would leave Kendall alone for her serious pregame preparation: watching YouTube clips of all-star scorers, Pittsburgh's Sidney Crosby or Chicago's Patrick Kane, visualizing their moves so she could use them in a game.

All this travel came with huge costs, up to $15,000 a season, Ahlise recalled. It wasn't just the hotel rooms or the wear and tear on the minivan. Players also needed to pay ice fees—which could add up to $4,500 a season alone. Kendall's parents worked hard, but they needed to get creative to be able to finance their children's love and talent for hockey.

Kendall's mom sold her diamond engagement ring to cover the ice fees one season. Another month, Kevin recalled the family could not afford to pay the electric bill and the company temporarily shut off the electricity. Ahlise boiled water on the gas stove so the kids could bathe.

When the orthodontist required payment as soon as Kendall's braces came off, Ahlise had an idea. Kendall would keep her braces on for an extra year so the leftover money could go toward a more pressing need: paying a professional strength and conditioning coach.

Kendall made her own sacrifices to excel at her sport. She never went to high school parties because she wanted to be alert for hockey practice the next morning. Besides, most of her friend community was made up of like-minded athletes. "I was okay with not being the cool kid in high school," she said.

In 2007, when Kendall was a sophomore in high school, USA Hockey started the first national team program for girls ages 18 and under (known as the U-18 squad). At 15,

The Coyne family Christmas card in 1998 from the Cammi Granato Gold Medal Hockey Camp. Kendall (seven years old), Bailey (two and a half) in Kendall's lap, Cammi Granato, Jake Coyne (four), Kevin Coyne (10).

Kendall was the youngest to make the team, and that was the beginning of years of international travel for her with the U-18 team.

Nearly every year, Kendall missed the first two weeks of high school to play on these teams. "It just took me being proactive with my teachers and explaining what I was trying to accomplish—my goal of wanting to go the Olympics and play for Team USA," she said. "It was hard, but it shaped me into who I am today."

Despite her experience playing internationally at the highest level, Kendall still experienced a setback. She had been recruited by top college hockey programs since she was in seventh grade and decided on Boston University.

But after promising Kendall a full scholarship, the coach inexplicably said it was no longer available. Kendall and her parents never learned why. Rather than go to her second-choice program, Kendall decided to reset. She did a post-graduate year at a boarding school in western Massachusetts—the Berkshire School.

"When Kendall wants to do something, she does it," her brother Kevin said. "Her response is, 'If it doesn't work, I'll try a different approach. Or I'll do it better.'"

That extra year turned out to be a gift for Kendall in many ways. She thrived in a private school environment. She healed from a recurring wrist injury to her dominant hand. And she practiced with both the boys' and girls' ice hockey teams, winning the New England Prep School Player of the Year in girls' hockey.

Kendall received a scholarship to Northeastern University in Boston. It was a program she would transform. Northeastern had never been to the NCAA championships before Kendall got there. In her senior year, she led the Huskies in what was then an eight-team tournament. Kendall earned the Patty Kazmaier Memorial Award as the top player in women's college hockey and set the Northeastern record for career goals at 141.

In the middle of her college experience, Kendall took a year off to train for the US Olympic team, which was preparing for the 2014 Sochi Olympics in Russia. This was a breakthrough moment. Kendall would go on to lead the team in points in their silver-medal effort, with two goals and four assists in five games.

However, Kendall was old enough not to be wowed by the big-time training experience and see beneath its cracks. USA Hockey, the national governing body for both the men's and women's teams, treated the men's national team like kings and the women's team like afterthoughts.

Kendall recalled how the US Olympic Committee paid a

core group of women's national team players a yearly stipend of up to $24,000. That was terrific. USA Hockey, however, paid them nothing. And unlike their male counterparts who had NHL salaries to fall back on, the women had to take on several jobs to afford to live.

When traveling to international competitions like the Olympics and world championships, USA Hockey gave the men's team a $50 per diem—a cash allowance to spend as they liked every day. The women's team was given a $15 per diem. During a residential training program, the women were not provided with post-practice meals, so everyone packed their own lunch. Another example of the inequity? USA Hockey would pay to fly a men's player's guest to the tournament, pay for their hotel and game tickets. The women's players did not receive such a benefit until 2019 (a year after the team won an Olympic gold medal).

This unequal treatment infuriated Kendall and her veteran teammates. Until then, they had mostly kept quiet, afraid that if they spoke up, USA Hockey officials would keep them off teams or find other ways to make their training difficult.

The US women's team won the 2015 World Championships. A year later, when she was eligible after her college career, Kendall joined veterans Meghan Duggan, Jocelyne Lamoureux-Davidson, Monique Lamoureux-Morando, and Hilary Knight in their fight for better working conditions. They had hired the same law firm that had helped the US women's soccer team in their own battle against the US Soccer Federation.

For nearly two years, USA Hockey didn't budge when it came to the women's demands for equal treatment. Then, the women realized they had leverage. The world championships were taking place on US soil. Weeks before the 2017 World Championships in Michigan, the players staged a boycott. Much like the women's soccer players before them, the leaders reached out to college players and told them to boycott, too. The women stood united.

Eventually, the US women's team got USA Hockey to offer travel provisions equal to the men's team, as well as higher stipends and prize money for winning medals. Crucially, they also secured injury and maternity protections for players in the deal. USA Hockey also agreed to put more resources into youth development programs for girls. Two weeks later, the US women beat Canada for the 2017 World Championship at the USA Hockey Arena in Plymouth, Michigan.

That momentum carried the women's team through the next year, when they won the gold medal at the 2018 Winter Olympics in PyeongChang, Korea. Kendall tallied two goals and one assist in the five-game tournament. Her family had traveled around the world to watch and celebrate with her. It had been 20 years since Kendall first held Cammi Granato's Olympic gold medal. She was elated to have her own but knew her work had only just begun.

Women still couldn't get any traction for a North American league that treated them professionally and paid living wages. In 2019, Kendall was playing with the Minnesota Whitecaps of the NWHL, a league of just four teams in the US. She was also working in community relations and fan development for the Chicago Blackhawks of the NHL.

In February 2019, Kendall was one of four women's players invited to the 2019 NHL All-Star game in San Jose, California, to demonstrate the different skills competitions to the fans—a kind of warm-up act. But then, at the last minute she got a call to be an injury replacement in the fastest skater competition. Without much time to warm up, Kendall skated first.

"Make it through the lap without falling," Kendall told herself. She knew how every girl and every woman who played hockey would be counting on her to put in a respectable performance. If she fell, it could set the women's game back years.

Kendall did better than just remain upright. She sped around the rink in a blinding 14.346 seconds, skating at a peak of 24 miles per hour, her edgework around the corners exacting.

She ended up placing seventh—one spot ahead of All-Star Clayton Keller, who finished last. She was less than one second behind the three-time champion Connor McDavid, who won in 13.378 seconds.

The celebration for the cause of women's hockey was very short-lived, though. Kendall went back to playing in a professional women's league without television exposure where she was the highest-paid player on her Minnesota team, making $7,000 for the sixteen-game season. The team and the league were so underfunded, they wouldn't even subsidize the $3 tape the players needed for their sticks. Kendall would sleep on an air mattress at a teammate's apartment, and, like many of her teammates, had to work other jobs. This reality made her realize just how unacceptable the state of women's professional hockey was.

"I just couldn't keep doing it," Kendall said, adding: "It was like, 'I'm not okay with this.'"

On March 17, 2019, Minnesota won the Isobel Cup, the NWHL championship. But Kendall did not stay in Minneapolis to celebrate with her teammates on St. Patrick's Day. She flew back to Chicago because she had to work the next day for the Blackhawks. Hours after winning the Isobel Cup, Kendall also had an important phone call to make and wanted to be home to do it.

When she reached her parents' house, she burst through the door, told them to hold dinner, and ran upstairs to call

Ilana. Kendall told Ilana just how profoundly broken things were in women's hockey. How could she fix it so that all of these talented players had a place to play?

"I could sense the hopelessness and the exhaustion," Ilana recalled.

We invited her to meet us at our home in New York City. That afternoon, we told Kendall she had to have every player behind her. There could be only one league in Canada and the US—and it had to have the best players. A united front. This was the strategy I used to unite two tennis tours to create the Women's Tennis Association (WTA) in 1973.

Kendall recruited players to join the Professional Women's Hockey Players Association. Ilana walked Kendall through the finances of starting a nonprofit organization, even taking her to a bank to open an account. Ilana introduced her to two top officials at the NHL, Commissioner Gary Bettman and Susan Cohig, the league's executive vice president of Club Business Affairs to discuss their operations.

Ilana and Kendall hired a full-time operations consultant, Canadian Hockey Hall of Famer, Jayna Hefford. She had starred in the old National Women's Hockey League, the Canadian Women's Hockey League (CWHL), and later became the CWHL's interim commissioner in 2018, until that league shut down in March 2019.

While they were searching for financial backing, Jayna, Ilana, and Kendall brainstormed a way to find games for the one hundred or so best women's hockey players in North America. They decided the players would host a mini tournament with four teams in different North American cities on several weekend dates. They would also put on youth clinics and hold autograph sessions for fans. They called it the "Dream Gap Tour."

The name was in reference to "closing the gap" between what a young girl and a young boy could dream about becoming.

In the fall of 2019, the tour stopped in Kendall's hometown of Chicago. At the beginning of the weekend, the players and coaches put on a youth clinic on the NHL ice before the Blackhawks game. For the cause of women's hockey, I agreed to participate in one of those fan intermission contests. I had three chances to shoot a puck through a cardboard cutout hole from center ice. I had never handled a hockey stick before.

During the first intermission, when Kendall planned to practice with me in the basement of the arena, she got called away for an interview. So her brother, Kevin, stepped in to coach me in the lower hallway of Chicago's United Center.

"How far is the goal from center ice?" I asked Kevin. He responded, 89 feet.

We practiced a few shots on the concrete. The stick was clearly longer than a tennis racquet. Armed with a basic 10-minute tutorial from Kevin, I walked out with Kendall in my specially made Blackhawks jersey onto a red carpet laid over the ice. I waved to the 20,000 fans who were banging on the plexiglass and chanting my name.

I hooked the puck short on my first try. On the second, I connected with the puck but sent it dribbling on its side halfway down the ice. Not good. I was furious. I was an athlete, after all. "OK," I said to the contest emcee through gritted teeth, "GIVE. ME. THE. PUCK."

I blocked out the fans and then cleanly wristed a shot that slipped through the cutout. The crowd went wild. "YES!" I yelled. What a rush.

Kendall jumped about six feet in the air, hugged me, and shook her head. "Is there anything you CAN'T do?" she said as we walked off the ice.

I had never picked up a hockey stick before this Chicago Blackhawks game in 2019. But Kendall's brother, Kevin, coached me, and on my third try, I scored during an intermission contest. What a feeling!

I was elated. And relieved. This was a good omen, I thought.

And then, five months later, the pandemic hit.

Even as other leagues found a way to play, women's hockey took a backseat. At the time, Kendall was having top-level discussions with financial and legal advisors, along with fellow US national team star Hilary Knight, and Canadian players, Sarah Nurse, Brianne Jenner, and Liz Knox. In 2021, Hefford got Secret deodorant to contribute $1 million to keep the "Dream Gap Tour" going.

"We had a call every single day at 9:30 in the morning, and Kendall was the player that was on it," Hefford recalled. "It didn't matter if she was at a world championship, or if she was training, she made the commitment to do the work and be in the grind. It wouldn't have happened without her."

From 2019 to 2020, Kendall was also working as a color analyst for the NHL's San Jose Sharks, and during the 2020–21 collegiate hockey season, she also did television work for NBC at Notre Dame University. She was putting her Northeastern degrees to good use: a bachelor's degree in communications studies and a master's degree in corporate and organizational communications.

In the early stages of developing the new women's league, we were still trying to locate the right financial backer for a professional league. We turned to another sport to do so. In 2018, Ilana and I had joined Mark Walter's Guggenheim Partners group and became minority owners of the Los Angeles Dodgers. In the next few years, Ilana and I talked to Mark and his wife, Kimbra, about making women's ice hockey their next best investment.

It finally happened in May 2023, when the Walters agreed to become sole owners of the PWHL, making a multimillion-dollar investment for a period of at least eight years.

There was one more task to complete before the league could begin: finalizing the contract between players and management (known as the collective bargaining agreement) that regulates working conditions and health insurance.

As president of the PWHL Players Association, Kendall was spending eight hours a day in negotiations with a core group of fellow players. Kendell would not budge on getting everything she wanted for her fellow players, especially housing stipends in addition to five-figure salaries. She was also eight months pregnant at the time.

"She's stubborn and I say that in the most positive way," Hefford said. "She just would not accept less than what she thought as players they deserved."

The group finalized an agreement in late June of 2023. On

July 1, Kendall gave birth to her son, Drew Schofield. (In 2018, she married Michael Schofield, an NFL offensive lineman for ten years, who had gone to the same high school as Kendall.)

Kendall's doctor told her she'd be cleared to play again in six months. Coincidentally, January 1, 2024, was opening day of the inaugural season of the PWHL. Kendall had a plan; she would be ready.

Fast forward to May 29, 2024, when Kendall lifted the first PWHL trophy, named after Mark and Kimbra Walter. The Walter Cup was made by Tiffany's. By design, it's exactly a half-pound heavier than the Stanley Cup that the men hoist after winning the NHL championship.

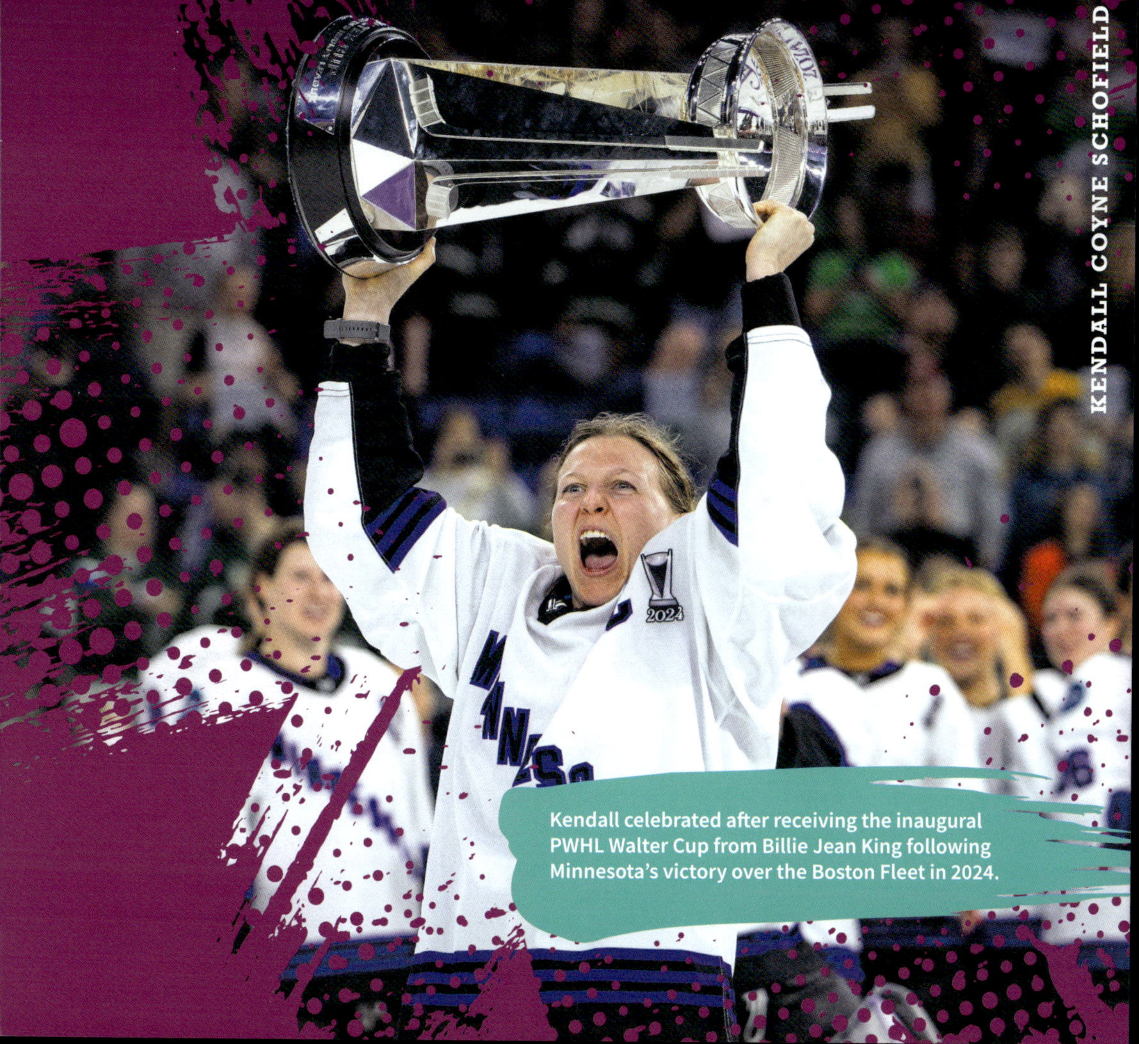

Kendall celebrated after receiving the inaugural PWHL Walter Cup from Billie Jean King following Minnesota's victory over the Boston Fleet in 2024.

Anything men can do, women can do better, of course. One part of the Walter Cup is made out of shattered glass, like the ceiling Kendall and so many female athletes have broken through.

After winning a second Walter Cup with the Minnesota Frost in 2025, Kendall said she felt like women had proven their skeptics wrong. "I think people are recognizing, respecting, supporting, and showing up for women's hockey like they have for men's hockey and men's professional sports for years on end," she said.

THERE IS A MOMENT IN EVERY GAME WHERE Kendall just takes over. It usually happens on a breakaway, when she flies past opponents. Other times, she anticipates mistakes so well, she pounces on them and scores.

"Kendall's just built differently," Minnesota goaltender Nicole Hensley said after a 2024 game where Kendall scored twice in the first 10 minutes. "She's our leader for a reason."

Kendall approaches leadership with a purpose. She schedules her time like an army sergeant. Practice. League promotion. Parenting. While she makes sure she signs autographs for young fans, sometimes, she told her mom, she worried that people might think she's unapproachable because she's so businesslike.

"No, Kendall, it's just that you don't have time for idle chit chat," Ahlise replied and later told me, "Everything she's doing is helping someone."

"I get that a lot. I'm focused. I'm committed. I'm dedicated," Kendall said. "You have to be willing to make sacrifices in order to accomplish what you want. And sometimes that means sacrificing a little bit of what might be fun to somebody

"…now they have this vision, they have this path. For them it's, 'I want to play in the PWHL.'"

Kendall in a 2025 game against the New York Sirens. She has always been one of the fastest skaters in hockey.

else. But for me, winning is fun, accomplishing your dreams and your goals is fun."

Her dream is not only to win trophies, but also to make sure the next generation of girls doesn't have to change into their hockey uniform in bathroom stalls rather than locker rooms or sleep on air mattresses rather than in their own beds.

In 2024, Kendall hosted her eighth annual Kendall Coyne Hockey Camp for 110 girls in Chicago. She started the camp because of the impact Olympian Cammi Granato's camp had on her as a kid. Kendall remembers one session of her camp very clearly. There, she addressed a room full of six- to ten-year-olds, starting with the basics.

"Do you guys know what the PWHL is?" she asked. In response, she received a chorus of "Duhs" and plenty of eye rolls.

"It's been six months of having this dream, and these six-year-olds are acting like it's been 60 years, and I'm the idiot in the room. Like, 'How do we not know what the PWHL is?'" Kendall recalled, laughing. "But they do know, because now they have this vision, they have this dream, they have this path. For them it's, 'I want to play in the PWHL.'"

To Kendall, nothing was ever a given.

"For a lot of the boys and the men growing up in the sport, they've always had the opportunity, they've always had the resources, they've always had the dream," Kendall said. "It's different when you've had to build the dream. You have a different perspective and an appreciation knowing you have to grind. Sometimes I look at it and think it would be so much easier if you didn't have to build the dream to get to the dream."

ICE HOCKEY

KENDALL COYNE SCHOFIELD

A star forward for Gotham FC, Midge helped lead New York to two league titles in three years, dazzling with her speed and agility.

CHAPTER 4

MIDGE PURCE, SOCCER

"RELATIONSHIPS ARE EVERYTHING"

MIDGE PURCE IS A SOCCER CHAMPION. SHE'S A TV producer, the star of her own reality show, the owner of a company, the founder of a nonprofit organization for Black professional soccer players, a negotiator, a commentator, a Broadway performer, a swimsuit model, a Harvard graduate, and an elected university officer. Midge is even a meme.

One thing she's not: a traditional role model for girls.

She posed smoking a cigar—gasp!—while cradling the 2023 championship trophy for the National Women's Soccer League in one arm and the Most Valuable Player trophy in the other. She won those trophies by assisting on two goals that led New York Gotham FC to its first title.

As soon as Midge posted the celebration to social media, she heard the criticism: Wasn't smoking a bad look for girls who see her as a role model?

Not if those girls want to win. Or if they know why she

smoked that cigar. It was a thank-you to her father, James Purce, who raised her and her older brother as a single parent.

As Midge tells it, she was a young girl when one Christmas she saw her father smoking cigars outdoors with the other men in the family. She thought it looked cool so she asked to try. Her uncles said no way. James only allowed her to hold it and light it that day but later allowed her to try one.

"My dad, like the feminist that he is, was like, 'You can have anything they have. You can do anything you want,'" Midge recalls. "He showed me how to chop it. He was like, 'Don't breathe in.'"

"That's how my dad has approached everything with me. It's always been that I can do whatever anyone else does, no matter that I'm a woman."

They planned the cigar celebration a long time ago when she first got into the pros, if she was ever to win a championship. When it happened, Midge was sending a private message to one person: "Dad, we did it."

Today, Midge is showing that girls can do anything boys can do—and oftentimes better. But she also wants to be clear that the reason she's playing soccer is not just to inspire young girls.

To her, that would be buying into society's narrative, one that the media and coaches help keep alive. Her point is compelling, as she explained it to me in an email that could be a book in and of itself:

"From an early age, girls are told—often in quiet, coded ways—that they're not strong enough, fast enough, or good enough. Confidence is treated as natural in boys but as a bold, almost rebellious act in girls. So, we build entire campaigns around telling girls they can—because the world has spent decades telling them they can't. And that 'not good enough' messaging doesn't fade as we grow up—it becomes more targeted, more persistent.

"Society creates this confidence gap. and then turns to the few women who manage to overcome it and says, your purpose is to fix it for everyone else. I reject that. While it's a privilege to inspire and uplift others, that doesn't have to be our purpose.

"Men have always been allowed to chase greatness for greatness' sake, but when women pursue greatness, it's expected to be in service of others. Why does my path to excellence come with a moral obligation?

"I love winning because I'm wired that way. I train relentlessly, push myself to the limit, and pursue championships because I want it—for myself. For that, I don't need justification. I'm not selfish. I'm elite."

Nobody knows this more than her father.

"She had a burning desire to be the best," James said. "If she scored one goal, she'd say, 'Oh, I should have scored three.' And I'm the one saying, 'Hey, that was a great goal, great game.' If she scored three, she'd say, 'I should have had four.' I'm telling her to bask in the win. No, she's pointing out how she can become better the next time out."

A mild-mannered stockbroker for Wells Fargo, James would listen as Midge sang to Miley Cyrus or chatted nonstop while driving thousands of miles together in their Dodge Ram 1500 flatbed truck from their home in Maryland to soccer tournaments in Boston, Chicago, Atlanta, or Miami. He would just chuckle, marveling at the funny, undaunted young woman he was raising.

He didn't particularly care for the nickname the girls on her 8-and-under club soccer team gave her—Midge—for her height. She was barely four-foot-nine at the time.

Midge with her devoted dad, James, who dispensed life lessons while driving in their pickup truck to soccer tournaments. "If you play big, you are big," he would always tell her.

He only calls her Margaret, Meg, or Mags.

"If you play big, you are big," he said.

That was the first of his many mantras.

Another: *"You don't go to practice just to practice. You go to practice to show the coach how much you've BEEN practicing."*

On that theme: *"Whatever you do when you're playing, no one should out-hustle you. It takes zero talent to hustle."*

Midge has followed all those Dad-isms. But this is the one that really rings true for her:

"ANY FOOL CAN TAKE A VICTORY LAP. YOU LEARN MORE FROM FAILING THAN YOU DO FROM WINNING."

For a champion who became an advocate for racial and gender equity while producing a groundbreaking reality TV show, Midge still points out her shortcomings. She has done everything except make a World Cup and a US Olympic squad.

"I do think I've become really good at failure," she said, laughing. "I get knocked down a lot and it hurts. And it has for extended periods of time. I think it's made me exactly who I am today."

Any fool can take a victory lap.

Midge Purce is a lot of things, but she's nobody's fool.

MARGARET MELINDA WILLIAMS PURCE WAS BORN in Silver Spring, Maryland, on September 18, 1995. Her brother, whom everybody calls JP, was three years older. Growing up, the two siblings would play every sport together: street hockey, kickball, snowboarding, baseball. They'd ride bikes and do daredevil jumps.

When James took his son to the park to practice for baseball, Midge insisted on catching the balls JP smacked into the outfield. She was four.

The three were a unit and James spent time shuttling them to their after-school activities. It was easier when both kids started playing soccer and then took karate. JP became a black belt in karate. Midge worked up to the second-highest level, brown belt. In elementary school, the children played musical instruments. JP played the saxophone. Midge played the violin. "Her recitals were a bit squeaky," James said, laughing.

When Midge was in fourth grade, Jim Bruno, a legendary high school soccer coach at the nearby Catholic school Our Lady of Good Counsel, watched her play in a local tournament. He turned to Midge's dad on the sideline and asked him whether Midge was planning to go to Good Counsel in five years.

Bruno could see that even as a nine-year-old, Midge played smartly and with pure speed. She could take any player one-on-one, faking them out, spinning and dashing to the goal before finishing the shot in the back of the net. Midge's agility was not surprising to anyone who saw her compete in figure skating, where she executed spins, jumps, and salchows, stopping the sport only when she got to high school.

No matter which events of hers James was watching, he would sit with a book in his back pocket. During practices, he would often sit in the truck reading spy novels or business books like *Seven Habits of Highly Effective People*. At home, Midge read books just as eagerly, from the Harry Potter series to *The Hunger Games* to *Uglies*, as she was drawn (and still is) to books set in fantasy worlds.

James originally bought the truck to take the kids camping, since the back could fit his fishing rods and gear along with the family's chocolate labrador. But by the time Midge was a teenager, the truck was serving another purpose: transporting the family to soccer tournaments.

"I'd lay a sleeping bag out the length of the back seat where she'd fall asleep, and she'd wake up maybe two or three hours later," James said. "She just talked the whole trip."

Her dad never discussed soccer strategy; he only cared

that she played hard. With his support, Midge was moving up in the club soccer ranks and reached the top club team in the Maryland area. Her coach, Shannon Higgins-Cirovski, was a member of the 1991 US Women's National Soccer Team that won the first Women's World Cup in China.

Midge credits Higgins-Cirovski for being a big influence in her career, and the two worked together in extra training sessions. James would flash the headlights on his truck to tell Midge to wrap up her workouts with Higgins-Cirovski when they went past dark.

"She's just, she's so intense, and she has a brilliant soccer mind," Midge said of Higgins-Cirovski, who would drill down on specifics, telling Midge how to perfect a move. "We would just keep going over and over it again until I got it."

By the time Midge was about to turn 14, she enrolled at Our Lady of Good Counsel, which was then a nationally ranked soccer program. If Bruno, the head coach since 1988, wasn't at the field early with his bag of balls, Midge would get frustrated. She was that anxious to improve.

"She's one of the fiercest competitors I've ever seen," Bruno said. "You had to work hard when she wanted you to work hard."

Midge was a sophomore forward when Imani Dorsey joined Good Counsel as a freshman defender. They had known each other already from area Olympic Development Program camps. As one of few Black players on the Good Counsel team, Midge took her under her wing.

Dorsey, who later became a defender for the Utah Royals in the NWSL, recalled how Midge always led with her big personality, on and off the field. "She could carry a room," Dorsey said. "She kept it fun and light."

In the Catholic league semifinals, Midge's team was facing

its archrival, a team that Bruno said had a history of trying to injure his players with targeted hard tackles. Sure enough, a rival player went to tackle Midge, and the two girls fell to the field. On the ground, the girl punched Midge across the face. "The whole stadium saw it," Midge's dad said.

Midge swung at her in retaliation, connecting multiple times.

Both players got red cards, meaning Midge was suspended for the finals. Our Lady of Good Counsel lost. The school also suspended Midge for five days because of its strict conduct policies. Her teammates rallied around her for not backing down, as did her father.

"My dad was so proud," Midge told sports media personality Katie Nolan on the podcast, *Casuals*. "He got me boxing gloves and the whole week he was like, 'Rocky!'"

As a junior and senior in high school, Midge was juggling high-level classes, SATs, club soccer, Catholic league soccer, and Olympic development training, a tough schedule even

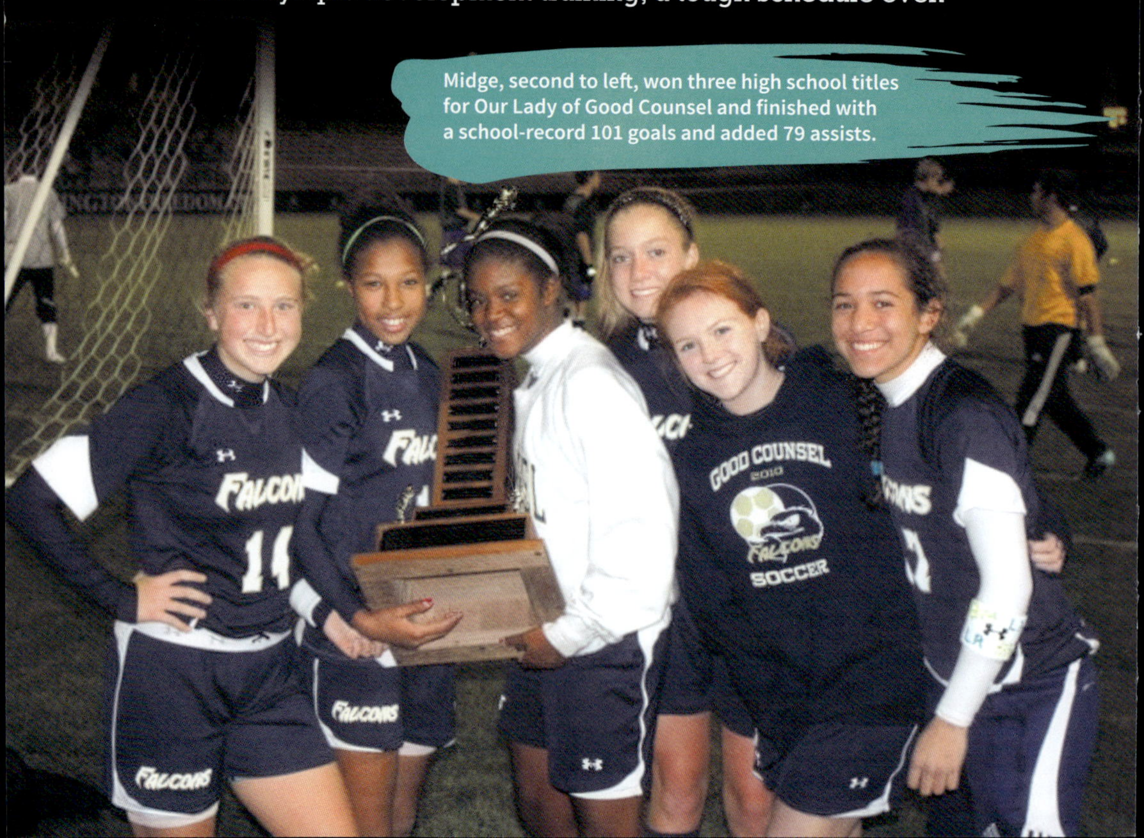

Midge, second to left, won three high school titles for Our Lady of Good Counsel and finished with a school-record 101 goals and added 79 assists.

for a high achiever. She made lists and wrote everything in her agenda book. Her father checked her grades; she said he allowed her to play soccer because of how she handled her academics.

"Meg has everything down to a science in terms of minutes and hours of her day, even today. Her time management is second to none, and she sticks to it," James said.

At one point, Midge was playing on three soccer teams: high school, club travel, and the US U-17 national team, for which she even traveled to Azerbaijan, a former Soviet Republic.

Midge finished her high school career with 101 goals and 79 assists, all while maintaining a 3.98 GPA. She made every league and state all-star team and was named the 2012 Scholar Athlete of the Year by the National Soccer Coaches Association of America.

She was considered the No. 1 recruit in the nation in 2012. All the top women's soccer programs wanted her: University of North Carolina, Stanford University, University of Virginia. When it came time to decide, her father was adamant that there was only one choice: Harvard.

"Stanford has a pretty good reputation, it's an excellent school," James said, explaining his thought process. "Harvard's number one in terms of an education, I thought it was second to none. So therein lies the decision."

Midge would be going to Harvard where the women's soccer team wasn't even nationally ranked and didn't play in a top-level league. How would US national team coaches see her play to assess her talent?

"It was very much a statement that she was going to Harvard, not a traditional soccer school," Imani said. "It was like, wow, she's paving her own path."

"If you're good enough," James repeatedly told his daughter about those national team coaches, *"they'll find you."*

Midge made herself extraordinary. During her freshman year, she would wake up before dawn for her own workouts, hitting the field at 4:45 a.m. before the football players arrived for their practices.

In 2013, Midge was the first player in Ivy League history to earn both the Ivy League Rookie of the Year award and the Ivy League Player of the Year award. She led Harvard to three Ivy League championships, culminating in a trip to the NCAA Tournament her senior year. She bookended her career by winning Ivy League Player of the Year in her final season.

Midge was drafted ninth overall by Boston's NWSL team, but her father worried that kicking a ball for a salary of $16,000 would be a waste of a good education. Midge had already ditched designs of becoming a doctor (organic chemistry was a killer of a class). To appease her father, she told him she would apply to law school. Her brother is a criminal defense attorney.

All James required was that she had a plan. In the spring of her senior year, she played for Boston's professional soccer team, the Boston Breakers, while completing her degree in psychology (and winning the Radcliffe Prize in 2017 as Harvard's top female student-athlete). She also studied for the LSAT.

Midge scored high, of course. But she believed she could have a more fulfilling career in soccer. However, it didn't help her case when the Boston franchise suddenly folded before the 2018 season due to money issues. All the players were drafted to other teams and within two weeks, Midge was on the Portland Thorns in Oregon.

She had a strong year with the Thorns and that helped her finally earn a spot on the US National Women's Soccer team.

In November of 2019, she made her first start for the national team, playing in a 6–0 victory.

And then came 2020. The pandemic shut down sports, and protests against police brutality were happening in cities nightly in June after the death of George Floyd. Many athletes were becoming activists.

That year, the NWSL was the first professional league to return to play with a monthlong summer tournament called the Challenge Cup in a sequestered part of Utah. Midge remembers it as a hot, uncomfortable, and frustrating time for the Black players, who then represented less than five percent of the league.

Outwardly, the soccer teams appeared to support the Black Lives Matter movement. Most teams knelt for the national anthem wearing Black Lives Matter shirts. But in one photo that went viral, three white players for the Washington Spirit were standing while the rest were kneeling: a picture of a league in disarray.

Off the field, many of the Black players felt like they were giving history lessons and defending their reasons for kneeling to white players. Anger boiled over when league officials put out a statement essentially saying that the players were in a good place.

"I will never forget. I walked off the field, and on my phone I had messages from almost everyone, at least one or two players almost from every team," Midge said. Black players wondered in outrage if she had seen the statement. "Everyone was just so upset with being spoken for in that way when it was so far from the truth."

The players needed a collective voice. Dorsey was not at all surprised that her high school teammate was the one to step up.

"She's like, 'I've been on the phone with this person, and that person.' She knows everyone, and she always has a plan of what to do," Dorsey told me. "That's what we needed at that point. Her vision and drive, when she sees an opportunity to make something better and bigger, that's really special."

Midge enlisted younger players like Imani and veterans like Crystal Dunn and Lynn Williams (now Lynn Biyendolo) to create the Black Women's Player Collective (BWPC). Midge was its first executive director. (At the time, 3.8 percent of the players in the NWSL self-reported as Black. In 2025, 12 percent of the players in the league identified as Black, according to the BWPC, as the league has grown more diverse with Black players from Africa joining rosters, as well as young US-born stars like Trinity Rodman, Croix Bethune, and Sophia Wilson.)

In the summer of 2020, Midge was pursuing other avenues of leadership. She had been campaigning for nearly a year to win a seat on the Harvard Board of Overseers, which is an elected group of thirty Harvard graduates who work with the president and the fellows of Harvard to oversee the university's operations.

She needed to go through a petition process just to be considered, getting more than 2,700 signatures. Midge, then 25, became the youngest person elected for a six-year term. She joined a group of overseers advocating for environmental causes and spoke for a younger generation. They had an immediate impact: in 2021, Harvard said it would no longer invest in fossil fuels.

"I could not be prouder," James said. "She came out of nowhere, and she campaigned and won the seat."

Midge was living up to the example her father set in his life: leading by helping humanity.

"I've seen him give a jacket that he had just bought to somebody who needed it more than him," Midge said. "I've seen him drive home, go get waters and other things, and go back out to give them to people."

Her own advocacy has always been close to home. While she was leading the BWPC and serving on the Harvard board, she was also taking up a decades-long fight in women's soccer for equal pay and equal treatment to what the US men's national team was receiving. Unlike the women, the US men have never won a World Cup or an Olympic medal.

The US women's national soccer team first made their demands for better treatment public in the mid-1990s when star midfielder Julie Foudy rallied her teammates to fight for equal pay and better working conditions—like playing on grass fields rather than dangerous turf fields and staying in nicer hotel accommodations. The women threatened to boycott the 1996 Olympics.

At the time, I had secretly advised Julie—telling her that to make the boycott work, she not only had to have her current team with her, but also the younger players. They needed a united front. We'd done this in tennis when I founded the WTA in 1973. Foudy and her teammates listened. And they won their fight. Change was just slow to come.

In 1996, the US women won their first Olympic gold medal at the Atlanta Games. Then came the incredible 1999 Women's World Cup. In front of 90,185 fans at the Rose Bowl in Pasadena, California, the US women defeated China in penalty kicks. That led to an iconic photo: Brandi Chastain ripping off her shirt in celebration to reveal her black sports bra and ripped abdominal muscles.

But even after these victories brought hundreds and thousands of fans to games across the US in the summer of 1999 and sparked the imagination of young athletes, the players still had to fight their own soccer federation to pay them what they were worth.

Two decades later, in 2019, women's national team star Megan Rapinoe was the face of the campaign for pay equity. All 28 members of the national team sued US Soccer on the basis of gender discrimination. Since Midge had not yet been named to the squad, she wasn't named on the lawsuit. But she was working behind the scenes.

She and Megan were the two players invited to the White House for Equal Pay Day on March 24, 2021. Of course, Midge went over her speech with her brother and her dad first. Her dad thought the metaphor she planned to use was over the top. She thought women would relate.

"When men began sports leagues, they were supported by billions in taxpayer subsidies," Midge said in the White House briefing room. "They were prioritized in media, and afforded time to grow. The investment was great, and the return was great."

Midge, dismissing her dad's advice, then added her colorful metaphor to bring the point home: "You would never expect a flower to bloom without water, but women in sport who have been denied water, sunlight, and soil are somehow expected to blossom. Invest in women, then let's talk again when you see the return."

Mic drop.

It wasn't until 2022 when the US Soccer Federation settled the lawsuit with the women. As part of the agreement, US Soccer had to work with player representatives on a collective bargaining agreement—the set of rules that would ensure that women not only were paid equally, but that they would have the same travel and childcare support so they could go to tournaments. Midge was one of the lead voices.

DESPITE HER MAJOR CONTRIBUTIONS TO SOCIAL change, Midge was unsatisfied with her career. In 2020, she had been left off the World Cup squad and told by the coach at the time, Vlatko Andonovski, that she didn't have the skills to be a forward. Midge would show him. When she was traded the next season to New York's Gotham FC, she scored nine goals and was a finalist for the league's MVP award—as a forward.

"I think I scored in almost every game for like six straight games," she said.

She made the next US national team, also as a forward. But in 2022, Andonovski told the media he was leaving Midge off the squad because of a "dip in play" and hoped that would motivate her.

Injury soon added to the insult. Midge strained her quadriceps and wasn't at full strength during the trials for the 2023 World Cup team. She was left off that squad, too. But when the US was playing the World Cup in Australia, she co-hosted a podcast with Katie Nolan, *The 91st Minute*, for the outlet, *Just Women's Sports.* When the favored US team shockingly lost in the Round of 16 and Andonovski resigned under fire, Nolan asked for Midge's reaction.

Stone-faced, Midge said, "I have none." The camera then cut to her cocking her head and flashing a sweet smile.

Her father loved it, texting her various memes people created captioning her knowing look.

"You're going to fail more than you succeed," James said,

another of his Dad-isms. *"It's just that that success is going to be seen, and no one knows what went into that one successful moment that everyone sees, all the hours, the pain, the suffering."*

It took weeks after the World Cup (which Spain won), but Midge was back on the pitch in the fall. She was finally healthy and led Gotham FC to their first championship.

"It wasn't this incredible year that everyone tries to surmise from this one little ending," she said. "You're a champion! It's like, 'Yeah, I am.' But gosh, I also tore my quad. I got cut from the World Cup team. I pulled my hamstring after I came back from that, pulled my groin."

But everyone will remember that she smoked that victory cigar, mimicking brash basketball champions like Michael Jordan (whose number 23 she wears) and Kobe Bryant.

In the busy weeks after collecting her trophies, Midge was already deep into planning another dream: a reality TV show. She had always loved watching shows like *Vanderpump Rules* and wanted to apply the concept to sports. Midge brought ten other soccer players to a rental house in Miami to film their workouts and their lives in *The Off-Season*.

Midge partnered with Alexis Ohanian, the founder of Reddit and the owner of two professional women's soccer teams. He had created a venture capital firm to give money to grow women's sports, and he immediately got Midge's concept. Ohanian also happens to be married to tennis legend Serena Williams.

Midge was an executive producer on set as well as the star. With Ohanian's support, she fired filmmakers during the production because they didn't buy into her vision; they wanted to stretch the truth in a way that would make players look bad. In addition to yacht and nightclub party scenes,

Midge struck a pose in 2023 when Gotham FC won the NWSL championship and she was named MVP of the game. She's smoking a cigar in tribute to her dad, James, who taught her that girls can do anything boys can do.

Midge insisted on showing discussions about serious issues for women's soccer—like pay equity and starting a family.

Midge left the rental house feeling like the cameras had captured so many stories that would hit home for non-sports audiences. A month later, in February and March of 2024, she played in a four-game tournament with the US National Team that ended in a victory over Brazil for the Gold Cup, an international tournament for the teams from North America, Central America, and South America. Everything was going according to plan.

And then, in the second game of the 2024 season for Gotham, Midge tore her ACL. That specific knee injury (the anterior cruciate ligament) always seems to derail female athletes at a higher rate than male athletes. The injury meant she would miss the entire 2024 season, including the Olympics.

After grieving, Midge saw it as an opportunity to be more hands-on editing the reality show. In October 2024, she and Ohanian released one episode a week of *The Off-Season* via the social media platform X, formerly Twitter. The first episode drew a whopping 2.5 million viewers.

The show was so successful, Midge formed her own production company around sports.

During that offseason, Midge spent quality time with her boyfriend, a Harvard graduate who is a hedge fund manager. She also got to hang out with her dad. When not traveling, she spent much of the time networking with television executives while also attending meetings for the Harvard board.

Midge embodies my core principle in business and leadership: "Relationships are everything."

She gets it. "I think that in my career, the way I've approached not just my on-field endeavors and goals, but also the way I've approached my off-field business has been primarily through relationships," Midge said.

"Almost everything that I have sought to do in advocacy has been a result of a relationship. Whether it's a relationship I had with another person, a relationship that I've had with teammates, or a relationship I had to the game itself and my experience."

AS THE 2025 SEASON DAWNED, IT TOOK MIDGE some time to work back into the starting lineup with Gotham. Gotham's coach, Juan Carlos Amorós, said that Midge was becoming a better version of herself, more calculating defensively and just as dangerous on breakaways with the ball.

By the second half of the season, Midge found her groove in the starting lineup. She helped Gotham beat three top teams to celebrate another NWSL championship. She entered the offseason as a free agent.

"Midge is a special player," Amorós said. "She's one of the players who's exciting for the fans, feared by the opposition, a joy to play with for her teammates, and a special person to coach."

And, he added, "She's known by everyone that she is not only talented for football."

In May 2025, Midge even made it to Broadway. She strutted on stage like she owned the Ambassador Theatre. Midge wore a stunning costume: fishnet stockings, black sequined dance briefs, a black crop top tied in a bow, and a bowler hat over her long blonde braids. In a slinky voice, she welcomed the audience of *Chicago* to a story of murder, greed, corruption, and treachery.

Area youth soccer players lined up in the Gotham FC tunnel to pump up the pros before a game.

"Everything we hold near—and dear—to our hearts," she said slyly before exiting stage right. But she wasn't done. Midge came back for the second act, sitting on the stage with the other dancers, her long manicured nails placed over her crossed legs. Later, she moved across the stage with the other dancers to play a reporter.

Backstage, the Broadway performers marveled at Midge's calm, admitting that they often get stage fright. Not Midge. She has already played for audiences larger than those at that New York City theater.

At a Q&A with fans after the show, she was asked if she ever had Broadway aspirations growing up. "Dad?" she called out to James sitting in the audience. He just shook his head and smiled.

"If you entered my home at any time, you'd hear my dad telling me to stop singing," she said.

Soon, Midge was signing autographs at the stage door, the first one for an awestruck Chloe Sneider, age nine, from Scarsdale, New York. Chloe had sat with her mom in the fifth row, mesmerized by Midge.

"She's my favorite player," Chloe said, smiling with a full mouth of braces.

Chloe pointed out Midge's speed, her grit, her goal-scoring, but most of all: "She just knows how to pass to people."

Midge knows that this, ultimately, will be her legacy in sport. Helping others. She learned this from the greatest relationship in her life: the one with her dad.

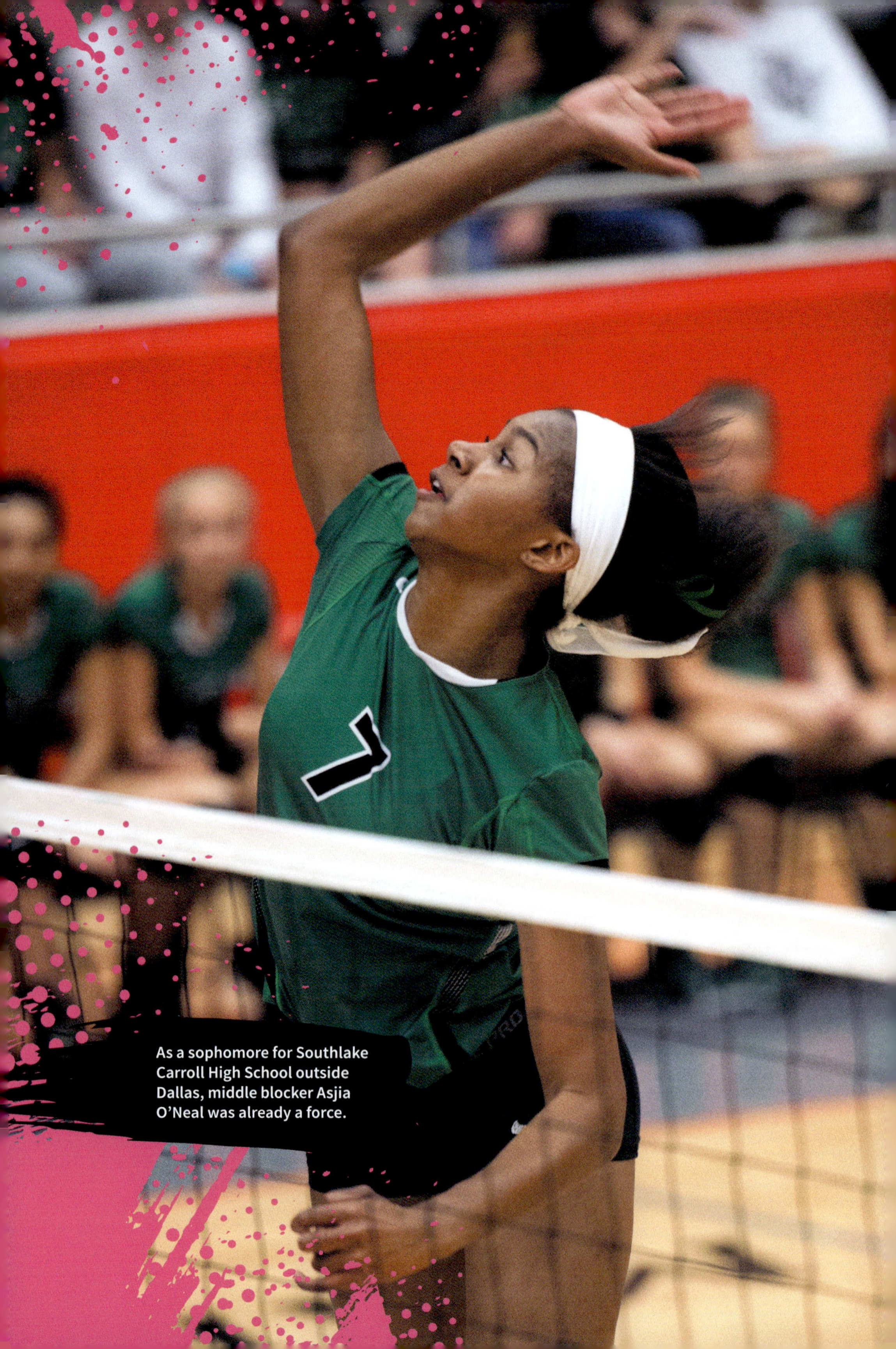

As a sophomore for Southlake Carroll High School outside Dallas, middle blocker Asjia O'Neal was already a force.

CHAPTER 5

ASJIA O'NEAL, VOLLEYBALL

"PERSPECTIVE IS PRICELESS"

ASJIA O'NEAL USED TO COVER UP THE FIVE-INCH scar in the middle of her chest where doctors twice fixed her heart.

She used to feel shame, not only for the scar's ugliness, but for what it meant: she wasn't always able to do everything her volleyball teammates did.

Now, when Asjia posts vacation pictures of herself in a bikini, she proudly bears the scar like a tattoo, a stark reminder of how she turned her struggles into success.

Her explosive talent and steady leadership enabled Asjia to become the first player to win back-to-back national volleyball championships at the University of Texas. She followed that feat by winning a professional title with Austin in the League One Volleyball (LOVB) Championship in 2025.

These days, Asjia is a member of the United States national volleyball team, training with the hope to make the

2028 US Olympic team. She is documenting her journey on social media, while talking honestly about how her life-threatening cardiac health issue caused her mental health to suffer. Her TikToks and YouTube channel make her part of a new generation of elite female athletes who connect with volleyball fans—especially young Black women like herself—to spur the fastest growing team sport in the country.

At six-foot-three-inches tall, Asjia also happens to belong to another elite group: children of famous professional athletes. Her father, Jermaine, was a six-time all-star forward for the Indiana Pacers of the NBA and played for seven teams in a 19-year career.

Her story is intertwined with her father's. She has always worn his number, seven.

After Jermaine retired, he built Asjia an indoor gym in their suburban Dallas backyard. He also built a 90,000-square-foot youth sports facility near the Dallas Fort Worth International Airport that was host to a top-level volleyball club where Asjia dominated. When Asjia needed open-heart surgeries, Jermaine used his NBA contacts to find her the best pediatric surgeons in the world.

"From a basketball standpoint, I thought winning a championship was going to happen," he told me about his career. "But I didn't realize the championship that I was winning was for my daughter."

Jermaine's role in saving his daughter's career, if not her life, is even more meaningful to him, considering that he never had a relationship with his own dad. Jermaine did not even meet his father until he was 30. Thirteen months later, his father died in a car accident. Painful memories of his father's absence inspired Jermaine, along with his wife Mesha, to fully commit to parenting Asjia and her younger brother, Jermaine Jr. Jermaine started his own sports agency and now represents his children and other promising volleyball and basketball stars.

Asjia credits her father for how hard she trains and the fierce determination she displays on the court. She even copies his full-throated yell after a winning point and listens to music to psych herself up before a game just like her dad did.

She credits her mother for teaching her sensitivity and sweetness and for being her best friend.

"Having my dad continuously speak life into me and my career as well as provide the tangible support pushed and encouraged me to keep going," she told me in an email. "I honestly never felt pressure from any of it, though. My dad helped fuel the fire inside of me to wanting to be the very best I could be and that's truly all I focused on. His support along with my mom's carried me through every challenging moment."

Asjia was two years old when doctors discovered she had been born with a leaky mitral valve that didn't close properly and sent blood flowing back into the heart. Twice, doctors told her she would never play volleyball again. They didn't know the true strength of her heart.

WHEN ASJIA WAS FOUR, SHE WATCHED HER DAD pumping himself up before games by blasting music in the bathroom of their house in Indiana. When the Jay-Z and 50 Cent lyrics got a little too adult for his daughter, Jermaine would listen on his headphones.

Asjia begged her parents for headphones of her own so she could bop around the house, too. Her mom then gave her a Hello Kitty boom box and a microphone, and she started singing and dancing.

You'd never know that Asjia was a shy girl—but put her on

a stage, and she felt right at home. Asjia's parents thought she was destined for a life in the theater. She put on puppet shows and plays for her mom and dad, who had built a stage with curtains for her on the second floor of their home. She took dance classes of all kinds—ballet, tap, jazz, hip-hop—and loved performing. Asjia even had a YouTube channel as a kid.

When Jermaine was traded to Miami in 2009, Asjia went to an elementary school specializing in performing arts and gymnastics. Mesha remembered when local executives asked Asjia to give a speech before a group of more than 300 adults. Her daughter breezed through it.

"My little baby is up here, speaking in front of all these corporate people," Mesha said. "She was a kid that would just do anything."

Around that time, Asjia also entered a school spelling bee. Jermaine came home from practice and saw her doing cartwheels in the living room and was concerned she would not be prepared. "Asjia, what are you doing?" he said. "This is no joke. You're going to be in a room full of people, and you gotta perform."

"Dad," she said, "I'm prepared, I'm going to win it."

Asjia did win it by correctly spelling "vegetable." Jermaine cried with pride. Despite not having a father in his life, he had done something right. "I've had to learn on the job," he said.

The one thing Jermaine knew about was how to play basketball, and he was excited when Asjia finally expressed interest in training with him the summer before she entered the sixth grade.

"I don't know why basketball because I never really enjoyed playing it," Asjia said, "but I guess I just wanted to find something for myself."

Soccer wasn't her thing. Maybe she could learn to like

basketball? "Then the first practice I went to, I absolutely hated it, and I did not show up again," Asjia said, laughing.

In that one workout with her father, she felt the sport was too physical. And too focused on individual achievement. She wanted to be able to move in coordination with teammates. A year later, she would get her chance.

With Jermaine nearing the end of his career, he and Mesha decided to choose a state in which to settle. They bought a house in Southlake, Texas, outside Dallas. He was playing for the Phoenix Suns at the time.

On the first day of middle school, Asjia was walking in the hallway when two eighth-grade girls approached her. They couldn't help but notice she was five-feet-eleven inches tall—in seventh grade.

"Are you going to try out for the volleyball team?" they asked her.

"I wasn't planning on it," Asjia said.

"You should really try out!" they said, leading her into the assembly and changing her life.

"I just loved volleyball immediately," Asjia recalled. "I loved that it was so cooperative, and you really needed every single person on the team at every single moment, and there's just always a lot of collaboration going on.

"And for someone who was super shy and just moved to a new state, new school, it helped me make friends a lot faster because we're always talking. We're used to working together, and it just kind of gave me that collective group immediately."

Asjia, however, was not particularly good at first. She made the school's "B team" because she was tall. But she hadn't yet mastered her hand-eye coordination.

She and her mom still chuckle about her first game playing

middle blocker, where Asjia stood waiting for the opposing team to serve the ball. When it sailed over the net, by instinct, she blocked it and celebrated. Her teammates, however, shook their heads in horror. In volleyball, it's illegal to block a serve at the net.

She had a lot to learn. And buy. Mesha bought volleyball clothes and kneepads and drove Asjia to every practice and game. Although Jermaine was working out of state, he was still motivating his daughter from afar.

"I would go on YouTube and watch highlights of my dad, just to invigorate something inside of me," she said. "I just remember always seeing my dad super-animated and aggressive and have really high energy."

One weekend, when Jermaine didn't have a game, he flew to Texas to watch his daughter play. He had ordered T-shirts for the whole family—her grandparents, aunt, uncle, and younger brother—that said in bold letters: "Asjia's No. 1 fan."

Asjia, like any self-respecting twelve-year-old, was mortified. "Dad, please take that off," she begged.

The entire family kept theirs on. And it became a tradition.

After the match, the middle school coach pulled Jermaine aside and said Asjia could be very good, but only if she also competed year-round on a club team.

The club fees were around $8,000 a year. Even though the family could afford it, her parents made sure Asjia understood that she had to make it worthwhile. "They were like, 'If we're going to make this financial investment, you have to be locked in,'" she recalled.

JUST AS ASJIA WAS STARTING TO LOVE THE SPORT, her progress came to a shocking stop.

She and her mom were shopping in HomeGoods one day when Mesha answered the phone. It was the doctor's office with awful news: tests showed that Asjia's heart valve was leaking. She would need to have open-heart surgery. Asjia broke down in tears. (For years, she never wanted to go back to HomeGoods, associating the store with that traumatic moment.)

"I always knew that I had congenital heart disease, but it was always something that was, 'You're good, no worries, see you next year for your appointment,'" she said.

While her parents tried to assure Asjia that everything would be fine, they were scrambling to get a second opinion. Although Jermaine was playing for the Phoenix Suns, his first call was to the Boston Celtics, his team from 2010 to 2012. That's because Boston had one of the top children's hospitals in the country. The Celtics' doctors helped arrange for Asjia to have surgery there.

"Right away," Jermaine said, "I knew that I was only in Boston for them to save my daughter's life."

Asjia, 13 at the time, recalled being scared to be put under anesthesia. Mom and Dad were at her bedside when she woke up. Jermaine told her how well the surgery went and that she'd be able to leave the hospital as soon as she was able to walk on her own.

The next morning, 24 hours after surgery, Asjia took her first steps. She bent over in pain, and Jermaine went to help her.

"No, Dad, I got to do this," she said. "I got to get better."

She remembered what her father told her when he played through knee injuries with the Celtics. Seeing him in obvious pain, nine-year-old Asjia asked him why he didn't just quit and do something else.

Jermaine had taken a deep breath, and responded: "Look,

you know you can't just quit things, right? You have to continue. Once you sign up for something and you love something so much, you got to figure out how to get through it and conquer what's bothering you."

With that same determined mindset, Asjia was able to leave the hospital in three days. "The doctor said that was the fastest he'd ever seen for any heart patient of any age," Jermaine said proudly.

Asjia's club volleyball team sent her pictures from their tournament in Colorado, lifting her spirits. They had brought her jersey, hung it up and took a team picture with it, as if she were there.

It took three months, but Asjia returned to them, better than ever.

- - - - ★ - - - - -

BY THE TIME ASJIA WAS A FRESHMAN, HER CARROLL High School team in Southlake was one of the top five high school volleyball teams in Texas. Her club team, where she played after the high school season finished, was also among the elite teams in Texas.

"That's when I realized, okay, everyone here is pretty good," she said. "I've got to put in even more work to separate myself from these people." That meant improving her strength and conditioning, in addition to her volleyball skills.

She began asking her dad specific questions about training and recovery—and how best to prepare mentally for matches. Jermaine did more than offer advice. He built a 7,500-square-foot gym in their backyard. It would also be a basketball court for their son, Jermaine Jr., who is seven years younger than Asjia.

Jermaine insists he didn't push his children to be elite

athletes but instilled in them the mindset that whatever they did, it should be at "100 percent" effort.

"I am very hard on them about process and what you should do and how you should do it based off not only the success that I've had, but also the failures that I've had," Jermaine said. "And Asjia has been a sponge."

Jermaine hired a coach to work in the private gym with Asjia and her best friend, Alina Lam, who was the setter on her club team. The setter and the middle blocker—Asjia's position—are the two who work together the most. Asjia would slide to one side of the net to prepare for a pass, then launch herself into the air off one foot and spike the ball over the net. Asjia's signature move was smooth and majestic.

Jermaine had invested more than $12 million of his own money to build a sports facility on the edge of the Dallas Fort Worth International Airport. In Asjia's senior year, he started a volleyball club there that he called Drive Nation. And yet, Asjia never got a big head from that.

"What separates her from other people is that she listens to other people, she knows how to motivate other people and get the best out of them," Lam told me about Asjia. "People respect her because she's never lazy. Her being humble is a big part of it."

Asjia went from being a promising talent to one of the top players in the country. The University of Texas at Austin offered Asjia a scholarship—when she was a sophomore in high school. She accepted.

"You started seeing her vertical [jump] and her speed and her agility get a lot better," the legendary University of Texas coach, Jerritt Elliott, told me. "We just saw all this potential in her that was pretty special."

But even as she was excelling in school and on the court,

Asjia was also hiding growing anxiety. She was scared about her heart. She was wired to push herself hard but worried that it would cause more damage to the heart.

At the time, her mother recalled, the coaches made it tougher on Asjia. Every Wednesday, the team had to run a timed mile. Mesha, five-foot-four, had been a sprinter on her high school track team. Asjia was always going to be slower because of her height—then six-feet. Her heart condition was impacting her endurance but not her game.

"She's the best athlete out there," Mesha said, "but then she's getting in trouble because she's not making this mile in the amount of time that they wanted."

Asjia would get upset with herself and uneasy because she wondered if people were whispering about whether she was fit enough to play. And that would lead to episodes of anxiety. Her mom would encourage her and try to distract her from thinking about her heart.

"Mental health is a much bigger topic now, but back then it wasn't," Mesha said. "So, I don't think I recognized the signs of her having anxiety. For me, it's just a kid that's scared. I should have gotten her therapy."

She added: "I didn't know, it was all new to me. I was kind of her therapy. That's why I would just encourage her."

Mesha and Asjia did not want to make a big deal out of what was a very big deal. "We both were like, 'Oh, she's fine, like she's got it.'" Mesha recalled. "Obviously, she wasn't right, you know, but she didn't want people to feel sorry for her, and I think neither did I."

Her teammates seemed to sense her unease. When they completed the mile run ahead of her, they began circling back to finish with Asjia. That's what she would have done for a struggling teammate.

Always encouraging, caring, playing music as the locker room DJ, Asjia led her team by example. She was both joyful and intense, just like her father.

Asjia played the most important position on her team with ferocity, leading it to the elite national high school tournament but unfortunately finished a disappointing second.

"I was like, 'I missed prom for this?'" Asjia said, laughing.

Asjia ended up going to a senior prom at another school with her club volleyball friends. Hanging out with a large group, Asjia met a boy named Carlos. They stayed in touch and six years later, became a couple. When they set up their apartment together, Asjia even put aside her bad memories and went to HomeGoods.

ASJIA ARRIVED AT THE UNIVERSITY OF TEXAS IN 2018 as the No. 1-ranked recruit for her position. But the Texas Longhorns had two older first-team all-Americans playing middle blocker in front of her, and Coach Elliott decided not to play her for a year. She'd be able to practice with the team but not play in matches, and therefore still eligible to play four collegiate seasons.

(This is known as "redshirting," a college sports term that originated with a 1937 University of Nebraska freshman football player who did not play in games but wore a red shirt at practices to identify himself.)

Asjia was crushed by Coach Elliott's decision. "Even if you know the people above you or ahead of you are better, you want to play. So, it just hurts you," she said.

Both Elliott and Jermaine told her to have patience, to trust the process.

"It's not your time, right?" Jermaine told Asjia. Then he

told her about his struggles in his early days as a highly touted teenage basketball star in 1996. After four tough years with the Portland Trail Blazers, Jermaine signed a contract with the Indiana Pacers. He started that year, and the next season, Jermaine won the 2002 NBA Most Improved Player Award.

Asjia drove herself to improve. "Asjia never took days off," Elliott said, adding: "I would put her in the very elite category in terms of the way that she approached the practices, the way that she prepared."

That was thanks to Jermaine's teaching.

"He is arguably one of the best fathers I've ever had in my program," Elliott said. "Just because of the lessons that he wanted Asjia to learn through sports, and he wanted it to be her own path."

When the redshirt season was over, Asjia went to her six-month heart checkup. The doctor bluntly delivered devastating news: she would have to stop playing volleyball if she wanted to avoid another surgery. She could, however, play a less strenuous sport—like cricket.

Cricket? Absolutely not!

Jermaine went to his NBA network once again. He called his former coach and mentor, Hall of Fame guard Isiah Thomas, and they worked to find a second and third opinion. Jermaine reached out to the Cleveland Clinic, who agreed to monitor her. Doctors said she didn't need surgery right away.

In the fall of 2019, Asjia was officially playing her freshman season. She was off to a promising start, but she sensed something still wasn't quite right with her body. She was quickly winded in drills and fought through fatigue and dizziness. Every player was wearing a heart rate monitor, and their rates were projected onto a scoreboard. This way, the staff could evaluate players' performances while primarily keeping an eye on Asjia. Seeing her stats only frustrated Asjia more as a competitor; she saw how everyone else was in the green (good) and only she was in the red (bad).

"Everyone knew about my condition, but sports is a culture where you're just told to push through everything. And this was something that I physically could not do, much as I was pushing," she said, adding: "Every day I just felt so much shame and embarrassment because I didn't want to have to think about my heart and I didn't want my coaches to have to keep pulling me in and out of practice . . . then I felt bad because there's other people that aren't playing games and they can get through the full practice."

The shame fed into her anxiety. "Looking back now," Asjia said, "everyone around me was very encouraging. So, it's sad to me that I felt that way, because no one was making me feel that way besides myself."

In the middle of the season, the Cleveland Clinic read her latest tests and told Jermaine and Mesha that they needed to come as soon as possible for a series of in-person appointments with four different doctors.

The initial appointments did not start well. Doctors agreed that she needed the surgery, including the one who said she should take up a different sport. That finally broke Asjia. Normally reserved and polite, she yelled in anger. Jermaine was in tears, and so was Mesha. He left the hospital for fresh air and prayed like he did when his son was born prematurely. He prayed Asjia would not only live a healthy life but also continue to play volleyball.

Jermaine, Mesha, and Asjia composed themselves and went to the final appointment of the day with the Chair of Pediatric and Congenital Heart Surgery at the Cleveland Clinic, Dr. Hani Najm.

Born in Saudi Arabia, Dr. Najm was a national tae kwon do champion in the 1980s. As an elite competitor, he uniquely understood Asjia's need to play volleyball. Dr. Najm told Asjia that she had outgrown the ring the Boston Children's Hospital surgeons put on her heart six years earlier. It was now choking her valve. She had been functioning on less than 60 percent lung capacity over the last year, maybe longer.

She could still finish the last four weeks of the 2019 season, he said, before having the surgery at the beginning of 2020. Most importantly, there was no risk of her dying on the court.

Dr. Najm took the sheet of paper on the examining table and then, with a pen, diagrammed Asjia's heart like he was drawing up a play. "He said, 'We're going to create a ring that is custom to you,' which ended up being the biggest ring that he's ever put on a human at the time," Jermaine said. "And then he said, 'You're going to come back and you're going to feel like a whole new person.'"

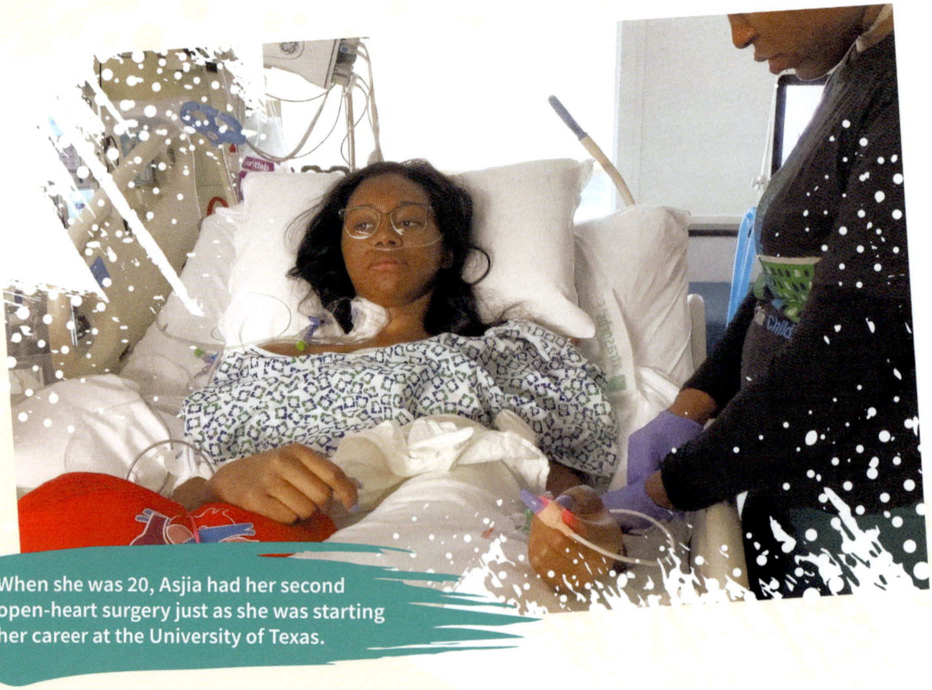

When she was 20, Asjia had her second open-heart surgery just as she was starting her career at the University of Texas.

When she returned for the surgery in January, she had added a new member to the group, one who had become family. Coach Jerritt Elliott wheeled her into surgery, fighting back tears. Then he and Jermaine and Mesha sat making nervous conversation in the waiting room. After five hours, Dr. Najm walked through the door and Coach Elliott will never forget what he said: "We've made her stronger than she was ever before, probably stronger than if she had a normal heart."

Asjia would still need to recover from the surgery that sawed through her sternum, leaving a long vertical scar and, at the bottom, three circular scars from surgical tubes.

She recovered gradually on her own in the spring of 2020 during the height of the pandemic. While many colleges had canceled their seasons, Texas and other southern teams returned to play in the fall. Asjia was back in Austin. Even playing with a mask on, she could breathe better than ever.

She had so much extra energy that she wanted to help others during this critical time in the United States. Asjia became a leader in the Black Lives Matter movement on campus. Together with her best friend and volleyball teammate, Logan Eggelston, they wrote the script for a 41-second video in which she and her Black teammates urged fans to support Black athletes off the court, too.

"All lives can't matter until Black Lives Matter," Asjia says in the video. She led a coalition of Black athletes from other sports demanding that the university change the names of buildings that had been named for pro-slavery figures from the Confederacy.

That 2020–21 season, Asjia was a dominant player in the Big 12 Conference, competing with Texas against other teams in the West, Midwest, and Southwest. By the next year, she was captain of one of the best teams in the nation.

But anxiety was creeping back. Her heart was fine, yet there were times on the court where she would still get winded and embarrassed. Would she be able to get through practice? She had been planning to win a championship since she committed to Texas, but would it happen?

She saw a university therapist, who helped her understand her anxiety. "I'm really glad that I did, because I still do now," Asjia told me. "I've realized the importance of having somebody that's completely a non-biased individual to talk to, to vent to, to get advice from."

As she felt more comfortable, so did her team. The Longhorns started coming together just in time for the postseason and Asjia was in fine form. Her teammates nicknamed her the "Slide Queen" for her graceful move in preparation for a kill.

Sure enough, Texas dominated in the 2022 championship match against the University of Louisville, winning in three straight sets.

"Once I was able to win in '22 it just felt like everything that I had prayed and hoped for and worked super hard for finally was here," Asjia said. "It made all the other dog days and really dark times worth it."

Asjia graduated with a degree in communications and nearly went on to play professional volleyball. But because of COVID, she had an extra year of eligibility. Coach Elliott convinced her to stay with the team and attend graduate school to receive her master of education in sports management. He needed her talent and, above all, her leadership.

The season started poorly (by Texas standards) with a 5–3 record. The Longhorns were figuring out team chemistry. After winning 17 of their next 18 matches, they arrived at the playoffs reinvigorated. Three victories later, they landed in

Asjia celebrated with her teammates when Texas won the Big 12 Conference championship on their way to winning the NCAA Championship in 2023.

the NCAA championship where they faced the overwhelming favorite, No. 1-ranked Nebraska. Earlier in the fall of 2023, Nebraska had broken a US attendance record for women's sports when their match in Nebraska's football stadium drew 92,003 fans.

The championship match held no such advantage for Nebraska. It was indoors at a neutral site in Tampa, Florida. Texas easily won the first set, then trailed in the second before Asjia, like all clutch athletes, came alive. She found her serving rhythm, delivering four straight aces which she would later describe as an "out-of-body experience." Texas won that set.

On the final point of the third and decisive set, Asjia served up another ace—a punctuation mark to her career.

"There's no better way to go out," Jermaine said.

Asjia's dad, Jermaine, and mom, Mesha (right, with flower), join family members to celebrate Texas volleyball Senior Night in O'Neal family style.

O'Neal family members and friends were there cheering in their custom Texas-burnt-orange shirts with white letters that made a play on words with the school's mascot, the Longhorns: "Hooked on Asjia."

This time, Asjia was not at all embarrassed.

She finished as Texas's all-time leader in blocks with 594. The championship, broadcast live on ABC in December of 2023, became the most-watched volleyball match in history, averaging 1.7 million viewers—an increase of 115 percent from 2022, when 786,000 people watched.

Asjia recalled how she watched the 2012 championship Texas team with star Black players like Khat Bell and how that inspired her. A decade later, she did the same.

"We are going to be able to land recruits for the next 11 years in Texas," Elliott said, adding: "There were lots of other kids that watched her and said, 'I want to be like her, a Black female in the sport of volleyball really doing some unique things.'"

- - - - ★ - - - -

ASJIA WAS CHOSEN BY THE COLUMBUS FURY AS THE overall No. 1 draft pick in what was then the Pro Volleyball Federation in 2024. But she spent the first few weeks on that Ohio team recovering from ankle surgery which set the tone for yet another career disappointment.

That spring, Asjia felt like she was on her way to the Paris Olympics, playing well in warm-up matches for a spot on the 12-person national team. But there was a lot of competition at her position. And then, at the Olympic trials, Asjia was beaned by an errant ball. She had a concussion which caused blurred vision and headaches. A freak accident ended her Olympic chances.

For the first time, Asjia took time off to rest without having to do any rehabilitation from surgery. In the offseason, she signed with another winter league, LOVB, as it began its first season. (My company, Billie Jean King Enterprises, invested in this league.)

Playing for Austin, Texas, (in her college town), she was surrounded by eight Longhorn teammates. Much like her freshman year in college, there were again older players at the middle blocker position. Battling minor injuries, Asjia did not play as much as she would have liked, but she celebrated enthusiastically with the championship trophy and her friends.

Elliott thinks Asjia has not even reached her potential. Volleyball players mature later, when they're 26, 27, and 28, he said. Asjia will be 28 at the 2028 Los Angeles Olympics.

"What makes Asjia so elite is that she's good at every skill set," he said. "She can be good in the front of the setter, she can be good behind the setter. She's an exceptional reader, she's an exceptional blocker, she makes all the little touches around the net. She's super steady emotionally," Elliott said. "But for her, she just needs to go play with the highest level, at the international level, to be able to get more experience."

In June 2025, Asjia did not make the national team, again beset by injuries and illness. She revealed this to her YouTube audience on the show *Roomie Diaries*, recorded with her friend and teammate, Logan Eggleston. Asjia said that her heart pumps blood slower than most people which explained the dizziness and other flu-like symptoms that bothered her during tryout sessions. She began to realize how much stress she still carried from her heart condition.

"I've had two open heart surgeries, so I should take myself seriously," she said. "I think just because when I was younger, for so long, like nobody believed me or ever thought I was taking it seriously, or people would be like, 'She just doesn't want to work hard.' That sat with me for the last 12 plus years."

She told her viewers that she is still trying to remind herself that she should not feel embarrassment or any pressure to keep quiet when she doesn't feel well: "I have paid my dues health-wise to be able to advocate for myself."

At six-foot-three, Asjia has a soaring vertical jump, giving her midair momentum to spike the ball. She helped her professional team, LOVB Austin, win a championship in 2025.

As a 15-year-old, Kelsie had a powerful leg kick pitching at a “Baseball for All” tournament in California.

CHAPTER 6

KELSIE WHITMORE, BASEBALL
"YOU DEFINE YOURSELF"

KELSIE WHITMORE LOVED THE GAME OF BASEBALL since she was old enough to hold a bat. Her father taught her how to throw, hit, and catch. She was a natural. Even at age three.

Although Kelsie quickly picked up the fundamentals—her dad Scott was a baseball coach and a middle-school gym teacher in their Southern California town of Temecula—she never seemed to want to play baseball with other kids. Her reluctance puzzled her father.

When Scott brought her to a softball game, she shook her head furiously. Nope. Not for her. Even when they watched Little League games, where sometimes there would be one girl on the field, Kelsie declined. Finally, her dad asked, "Why don't you want to play?"

"I don't want to put my hair up in a ponytail," Kelsie said.

She loved her chestnut brown hair flowing down the

middle of her back. It was her signature. Most days she'd forget to brush it, racing to school looking like a wild child. The hair on her head was hers, and she didn't want anyone to tell her what to do with it.

"But Kelsie," her father told her, "You can wear your hair any way you want!"

So with a cap on her head and her hair tucked loosely behind her ears, six-year-old Kelsie finally joined a team. Over the next 20 years, she would redefine what was possible for girls playing a sport that previously had been exclusively for boys.

Kelsie's talent enabled her to play on boys' teams, becoming a Little League All-Star and advancing to play travel ball. In high school, she also played for the boys' team. At 17, she was a starting outfielder for a men's minor league professional team. At 23, she became the first woman to sign with a Major League Baseball partner, the Atlantic League, pitching and playing outfield for the Staten Island FerryHawks.

At each stage of her groundbreaking journey, Kelsie heard critics question her choice to play baseball. She was constantly told she should be a softball player. But at her core, she was a baseball player.

"You chase your whole life being someone you're not," she told me, "And then eventually you're like, the only person I should be chasing is myself."

Kelsie Ann-Gamboa Whitmore is the proud daughter of a mom born in the Philippines and a father born in Iowa. Being biracial was never an issue for Kelsie. Perhaps that's because, in the game of baseball, she could be many things at once. A pitcher. An outfielder. A batter who could hit from both sides of the plate.

Today, Kelsie is a trailblazer using her leadership to

Kelsie first dreamt of playing in the big leagues while watching her hometown San Diego Padres with her brother Matthew.

'Hey, if you can hit this fastball, but you have to hit lefty, and I'm throwing as hard as I can righty, then I owe you this much money.' Baseball just was everything."

Living in Southern California enabled Kelsie and Matt to play baseball outdoors almost daily. When they couldn't play on a field, they created their own baseball diamond. Where would first base be? The drain in the street. Second base? The trash can lid. The siblings had a portable pitcher's mound, and Kelsie and Matt dragged it into the street. Their dad also purchased a machine that tossed pitches they could hit or fly balls they could catch.

When it rained or got dark, she and Matt placed pillows on the living room floor for bases, and the step-up to the dining room became the outfield. They took down picture frames hanging on the walls after their mom got mad when they cracked one.

Playing on boys' teams, Kelsie never felt different because of her gender or her hair. In the early 2000s, boys had long hair, too. Besides, no one on her team cared because she was *good*. At the end of the season, coaches would select the top players in the league. Officials would come overnight to plant a sign in her front yard, signifying she made the all-star team. The whole neighborhood knew they had a remarkable talent living on their block.

When Kelsie was 12 and still the only girl on her travel team, the kids and parents flew to the Baseball Hall of Fame site in Cooperstown, New York, for a summer youth tournament. Kelsie hit a grand slam off her friend, Simon, making him cry. They still laugh about it today.

The next year, Kelsie joined a group of girls' all-stars from around the country who traveled to tournaments to play against boys' teams. They called themselves the Dream Team and, at 12, Kelsie was one of the youngest players. Her father, Scott, recalled that one boys' team refused to take the field at a tournament in Michigan. The boys worried that if they lost, they would be humiliated. Or if they won, it would not mean anything; they beat a girls' team.

"The tournament director said, 'Get on the field to play, or get the hell out of my tournament,'" Scott recalled.

The team started their best pitcher and destroyed the Dream Team.

But not all teams felt threatened. After the Dream Team beat a boys' team from Colorado, at a tournament, the boys welcomed the girls to their campsite, cooked them dinner, and asked to exchange uniforms.

Many people support girls playing baseball, Scott said. "The difference," he added, "is the haters are just louder."

Some haters were close to home. At a year-end picnic for

teachers and administrators, a high school athletic director from a rival school approached Scott and Kelsie. Kelsie would be starting high school the next year.

"You know," the athletic director said, "she's never going to make it in baseball." He suggested, of course, that she just play softball.

Scott was stunned. He turned to Kelsie and told her that her mom was calling for her, motioning her to leave. Of course, Kelsie's mom hadn't actually called, but he didn't want Kelsie to hear what he said next.

Scott ripped into the administrator. "Don't you EVER tell my daughter she can't do anything!" he yelled, adding a couple of salty words to make his point.

He never spoke again to that athletic director, who himself oversaw successful girls' sports teams. At the time, the man's teenage son had pro baseball aspirations. His son never made it.

People who questioned Kelsie were questioning Scott, too.

"Until you've been a parent of a child that isn't in the bubble of norm, they don't get it," Scott said with a sigh. "You know those parents are saying that we are forcing them to do this. This was completely brought on by Kelsie's desire, and we just funneled it and helped direct it."

Kelsie was reluctant to share her goals of playing professional baseball publicly again. When asked about her career aspirations, she would say coach or personal trainer.

"It only fired me up, but I never stopped pursuing it," Kelsie said. "I just stopped sharing my dreams because there are dream crushers out there. Some things you need to keep in the privacy of your heart."

There was one place where she felt comfortable: with other baseball-playing girls.

In 2011, when she was 13, Kelsie took part in a girls' clinic in Compton, California. Justine Siegal, a Cleveland native who had fought to play on boys' teams throughout her career and had risen to be the first female coach of a professional men's baseball team, founded a nonprofit organization in 2010 called "Baseball for All." The goal: provide opportunities for girls to play and coach in baseball.

Siegal knew immediately that Kelsie had the talent to make it as a professional.

"Kelsie was, by far, the best player there," Siegal told me. The camp grew each year, and Kelsie participated again when she was 15. By then, they had enough players to field three different teams.

After the camp, Kelsie went back to playing with boys' teams. She was always a shy person, very much like her mom, Mirasol. Being the only girl on boys' teams often made her feel more isolated.

"Growing up, the hardest thing was learning how to ask, 'Hey, do you want to play catch?'" Kelsie recalled. "That was my biggest fear, and it sounds so silly now."

Kelsie said she felt embarrassed, not wanting to inconvenience people by asking where the girls' restroom was to change into her uniform.

"I was just so shy all the time," Kelsie recalled. "I didn't know how to stand up for myself. During my teenage years, I felt very lonely because I didn't know how to be my own person."

She talked to herself. A lot. "I tricked myself enough that I became confident," Kelsie said. "And even though I wasn't. Even though internally I was scared, I was nervous, I was worried, I was insecure, I was all these doubtful things, I would trick myself to being like, 'No, you know what you're doing. You're here for a reason.'"

What set Kelsie apart then and at every stage in her career was her work ethic. She loved to play the game, but she also practiced hitting for hours in the batting cages, did her strength training with bands, and took special care of her glove like it was a cherished family member. No one was allowed to put their hand in it.

Kelsie played on the freshman boys' baseball team for Temecula Valley High School as an outfielder and a relief pitcher. As a sophomore and junior, she played on the junior varsity boys' teams. She made the varsity team her senior year.

At 16, Kelsie was chosen to play for the US women's national baseball team. Although women's baseball wasn't an Olympic sport, women on the team could participate in a World Cup and other international competitions. During high school and throughout the summers, Kelsie traveled with her teammates to play in Korea, Mexico, Canada, and Japan. In 2009, Japan started a professional women's baseball league that operated for 12 years.

Despite her baseball prowess, Kelsie did not specialize in one sport. That was her dad's idea. As a middle-school physical education teacher, Scott stressed cross-training for all his students. He created a fitness contest and put the leaders on a board: Kelsie led the entire school. His daughter picked up different sports so quickly; it was as if her body and mind already knew what to do.

Kelsie played golf in high school, developing a swing so powerful she could drive the ball more than 300 yards. Kelsie also played soccer as a midfielder balancing speed and sharp passing skills. Still, Kelsie worried about injuring her right pitching arm.

She told the soccer coach that she wanted to focus on baseball as a senior. He begged her to stay and play goalie which was a bit safer. Kelsie had never played that position, but she signed up for coaching sessions. She was such a natural athlete that she won top goalie honors in the league.

Like most high school seniors, Kelsie started thinking of her future. To her, that only involved one career: baseball. Her dream found a sponsor. The noted film director Francis Ford Coppola owned a vineyard in Sonoma, California, and a minor league baseball team, the Sonoma Stompers. (So named because grapes are "stomped" in the wine-making process.)

Coppola grew up playing family baseball games with aunts and female cousins and felt baseball was supposed to be coed. When Coppola wanted to form a team that included the country's top female players, he called Justine Siegal, the founder of Baseball for All. She recommended Kelsie.

Team officials of the Sonoma Stompers traveled south to Riverside County to watch Kelsie play in a high school game to see if she was legit. When she was at bat, the pitcher—intentionally or not—threw an 83-mph fastball that drilled her in the ribs. Kelsie had never felt such extreme pain. She trotted to first base for the automatic walk, choking back tears. Then she coughed up blood.

Kelsie waved off her concerned manager, insisting she stay in the game. Meanwhile, she was screaming inside: "Show no weakness! Show no weakness!"

Siegal understood that refrain all too well. "She had no choice. She had to keep going," she said. "It would have been an excuse of, 'See, girls will get hurt. We can't have them play with men.' When you are a girl playing with boys, you cannot show weakness, no matter how much it hurts."

Kelsie aced the tryout and, for her summer job, signed with the Stompers of the independent Pacific Association of Professional Baseball Clubs. She started her first game in the outfield on July 1, 2017, alongside another woman, Stacy Piagno, a 25-year-old pitcher from Florida. When catcher Anna Kimbrell joined the team, she and Kelsie became the first female pitcher-catcher combo (known in baseball as a "battery") to start a professional men's baseball game.

But this wasn't the first time women played professionally with men. That honor of "first" belongs to Toni Stone who, in 1953 at age 22, signed with the Indianapolis Clowns of the Negro American League. The Clowns' owner, Syd Pollack, sold Stone's contract for the 1954 season to the Kansas City Monarchs in the same league. In her place, he added two more women—pitcher Mamie "Peanut" Johnson and then Connie Morgan at second base. The three were pioneers.

From the beginning, the rules of baseball—written by men—were quite clear: girls were not supposed to play the sport, at least according to the rulebook written by sporting goods mogul Albert G. Spalding in 1911. In *America's National Game*, Spalding wrote that women could cheer but not play: "she may take part in grandstand, with applause for the brilliant play, with waving kerchief to the hero." He concluded: "Base Ball is too strenuous for womankind."

Seriously?

But women had been playing baseball since 1866, when students at the all-woman Vassar College in New York fielded two teams. The movement spread to other all-woman colleges in the Northeast. In 1867, two years after the Civil War ended, a team named the "Dolly Vardens" made up of all Black players from Philadelphia became the first professional women's team. (The team's name came from an 1841 Charles Dickens novel, *Barnaby Rudge*, in which the character Dolly Varden wore brightly colored dresses that then became a fashion trend around the 1860s.)

During World War II when men were fighting overseas, a women's baseball league flourished, immortalized in the 1992 movie, *A League of Their Own*. The All-American Girls Professional Baseball League ran from 1943 to 1954, growing from a niche entertainment venture for baseball-starved fans during the war to a veritable platform for women in the sport. But only white women. And they had to wear skirts.

When the league disbanded, girls seemed to disappear from baseball for the next two decades, but that didn't mean they stopped playing. In 1972, Maria Pepe, a 12-year-old from Hoboken, New Jersey, was one of the top players and the only girl on her Little League team, the Hoboken Young Democrats. But after playing in three games, the Little League leaders forced her off the team because of her gender.

Pepe sued, backed by the National Organization for Women (NOW). During the 1973 hearing before the New Jersey Division on Civil Rights, Little League officials claimed that the sport was dangerous for girls. If they got hit in the face, it would "ruin them for marriage." (Actual testimony!) And in testimony that was completely baseless medically, an official claimed that if girls were to be struck in the breast, it would cause breast cancer. Unbelievable.

Pepe and NOW won the landmark case. Sylvia Pressler, the hearing officer who later became a New Jersey state judge, issued this famous ruling: "The institution of Little League is as American as the hot dog and apple pie. There's no reason why that part of Americana should be withheld from girls."

Still, the sweet victory had a bitter aftertaste. Little League of America was ordered to make the sport accessible to girls. Instead of publicizing that girls could now play on boys' teams, they created a new league that they promoted: softball for girls.

Softball's field dimensions are smaller (bases are 60 feet apart; 90 feet apart in baseball), and the ball is bigger (12 twelve inches round versus nine inches round). Softball pitchers throw underhand, so the ball comes in at a different angle than in baseball. Softball uniforms are generally more fitted than baseball uniforms, and the girls wear visors, not caps.

Softball? "It's the last thing I'll ever do," Kelsie said as a high school senior. "The whole hair up, braided, makeup vibe. I fought it a lot, like I would be losing my identity."

After assessing her college options—she was offered a scholarship from a small college for soccer but not to play baseball on a men's team—Kelsie agreed to consider softball. Having never played the sport, she went to a tryout camp where softball coaches from the University of Texas, University of Hawaii, and California State University at Fullerton followed her every move. Granted, her moves were raw, but the coaches saw potential.

Kelsie made it clear that she still wanted to play baseball in the summer and, ideally, also practice with the baseball team when she could. Cal State Fullerton softball coach Kelly Ford was eager to oblige. She had the baseball coach, Rick Vanderhook, talk to Kelsie, and he showed her the team's facilities.

Ford wanted Kelsie for more than just her athleticism. "She just had this wisdom about her, this maturity," Ford said. "She was really passionate about her story, and you couldn't help but want to be a part of this story."

For Kelsie, playing a similar ball sport kept her instincts sharp. She also had another motive.

"There was this part of me that was tired of not fitting in," Kelsie said. "Maybe if I played softball, I would fit into something. Maybe I'll learn to be able to talk to people and make a conversation. Maybe it won't hurt."

It hurt. The juniors and seniors on the team teased her for being "the baseball girl." She shook her head, recalling: "It was like, 'What do I need to do to be enough for people?'"

Finally, at the end of her sophomore year at Cal State, Kelsie just embraced her outsider status. She told Coach Ford, "Listen, if I'm going to play here, I need a baseball hat. Next, I need baseball pants."

Ford immediately walked over to the baseball equipment room to get her pants, jersey, and a baseball cap. As Kelsie felt more confident in her appearance, her softball teammates started to accept her.

"Eventually, they realized, 'That's Kelsie being Kelsie,'" she said. "I did get a few dirty looks when my hair was down, and, honestly, I did not care. That's when I started to turn that fire in me into fuel."

It would be easy to say the uniform caused a magical improvement in her game. But in reality, Kelsie had finally figured out the game of softball. Hitting a rising fastball or a changeup was a challenge because an underhand pitch moves in the opposite direction as an overhand baseball pitch. Earlier in her softball career, she would take huge swings and strike out. But the coaches knew once she got her timing down, it would be lights out.

As a freshman and sophomore at Cal State Fullerton, she got into games as a pinch runner. By her junior year on the softball team, she started in right field and was named to the All-Big West Second Team.

Because the COVID pandemic shut down her senior season after 24 games, all athletes got an extra year of eligibility. Kelsie decided to stay at Cal State Fullerton and get a master's degree. She had already earned a bachelor's degree in kinesiology in 2020, and she would earn her master's in instructional design and technology two years later.

In 2021, Kelsie recorded one of the top offensive performances in the history of Cal State Fullerton's softball program, with an 18-game hitting streak and a slugging percentage of .829. She finished with a league-best 13 doubles, 45 runs, and 12 home runs. And she made no errors in right field. In only her fourth season playing the sport, Kelsie became the Big West Conference Field Player of the Year, leading the team to a 38–15 record.

In one memorable game, Kelsie dramatically crushed a pitch to left field, sending it 60 feet over the fence, one that was 300 feet from home plate. "It dented our scoreboard. I don't know if that had ever happened before," Ford recalled.

While Kelsie left that literal impact on the program, it was her work ethic and the little things she did that cemented her legacy. Local girls would come to games hoping to emulate her. One girl, Maggie Paulovich, even wore her long hair tucked behind her ears under a baseball cap like Kelsie. Several years later, Maggie joined Cal State Fullerton's softball team and was chosen to play for USA Baseball.

Kelsie's coaches marveled at Kelsie's meticulous 20-minute pregame routine. She would attach a strengthening band to the dugout fence and complete repetitions (athletes call them "reps") of every set, never once taking a shortcut.

"Nobody took the outfield like Kelsie Whitmore," Ford said. "From the first step out of the dugout, she would take a full sprint to her spot. Everybody else takes a good jog. But she just has so much intent. These are the kind of intangibles that you can't teach. You can't teach swag."

Looking back, Kelsie was appreciative of the softball experience. But she was also anxious to get back to her dream.

The same discipline she had on the field transferred to her job search. Kelsie had no agent then, so she spent hours sending emails and highlight videos to minor league coaches asking for tryouts. She got used to rejection. She lived on an air mattress in an apartment in Pittsburgh with three other guys as they played semipro baseball. Kelsie had entered what she now calls, "Grind Mode."

Then, on April 8, 2022, she got a life-changing call from Gary Perone, the general manager of the Staten Island FerryHawks of the Atlantic League.

Kelsie became an overnight media sensation for this minor league team, whose ballpark is up the block from the Staten Island Ferry Terminal. After Kelsie patiently sat for media interviews, she spent time asking questions of her teammates and coaches, like former Major League pitcher, Nelson Figueroa. She'd be in the bullpen with Figueroa, then the FerryHawks' pitching coach, asking him about release speed and whether she should throw a knuckleball.

The transition to facing far faster pitches as a batter and elite hitters as a pitcher was challenging. In two seasons, she played in 56 games, including pitching 22 innings as a reliever, allowing 27 earned runs. At the plate, she had 1 hit, 3 walks, scored 3 runs, and struck out 33 times.

Kelsie admitted that she struggled with anxiety whenever she came to bat, worried that whatever she did would reflect poorly on her gender.

"I'm like, 'I need to be perfect. I can't mess up,'" she said.

In order to prove herself, she needed to hit to stay in the lineup. It was a vicious cycle. And like so much about sports—and life—you need to have the reps to get better.

In 2024, Kelsie continued to pursue her dream back on the West Coast. She got an offer to play in California, with the Oakland Ballers, who played in the Pioneer League. She played 13 games, starting five as a pitcher, and became the first woman to start a game in the league.

Kelsie vowed to become stronger. She maintained a rigorous workout regimen that often consisted of six-hour gym sessions. She would travel for throwing sessions at minor league parks. Her brother, Matt, would be her throwing partner.

In 2025, she was invited to a spring tryout with a professional team in Mexico. Kelsie thought she had played well enough to make the team. Unfortunately, they cut her. They didn't tell her outright it was because she was female. Instead, they "beat around the bush," she told me in an email, giving reasons like "we don't want you to get hurt" and "we can't keep you because of political reasons." Kelsie said it was pretty clear she didn't make the team because of her gender.

Angry and frustrated, Keslie seriously considered quitting baseball and giving up her dream to play professionally. She began searching for boring office jobs. A devout Christian, she prayed for a sign.

A week later, in the summer of 2025, Kelsie got a call to come play with the Savannah Bananas, a different and wildly popular baseball team in the United States. Wearing bright yellow baseball uniforms, the players put on exhibition games with creative baseball rules and choreographed dances to spice up the action and involve families. When Kelsie took the mound in front of 40,000 fans at Petco Park in San Diego, her hometown ballpark, she was beyond thankful. She recorded her first strikeout and first win as a Savannah Banana.

Kelsie celebrated her first professional strikeout with the Savannah Bananas in front of a sold-out Petco Park in 2025.

"I went from thinking my career was over to living out my childhood dream-moment."

"I went from thinking my career was over to living out my childhood dream-moment," she said in an Instagram video.

Her other dream was soon to come true. Kelsie was the first player drafted in the Women's Pro Baseball League (WPBL), chosen by San Francisco. The league was cofounded by Justine Siegal with businessman Keith Stein. When the WPBL began play with four teams in 2026, Kelsie was already an ambassador for the game.

The feeder system for girls in baseball looks completely different today than it did when Kelsie was growing up. There are more than 50 girls' teams that play in a national summer tournament that Siegal runs, from 8-U teams up to 18-U. The National Federation of State High School Associations' sports statistics in 2025 showed 1,381 girls playing on high school boys' baseball teams across the country. Roughly 100,000 girls played on Little League teams.

For the first time in 2024, Major League Baseball featured female players, including Kelsie's avatar, in the video game *MLB The Show*. She was also featured in a film about women's professional baseball called, *See Her Be Her*. (I was proud to be an executive producer on that documentary.)

The opportunities for girls in baseball, however, are still limited because colleges don't offer girls baseball scholarships.

"This is a social justice issue that girls are being told they can't play baseball or are being shown a different path before being given the opportunity to choose," Siegal said.

If girls had a path to college and the pros or they had more role models like Kelsie, they would be able to field competitive teams. They wouldn't have to justify themselves to men in the sport. They could play with freedom.

"When I watch Kelsie play with men, I see determination,"

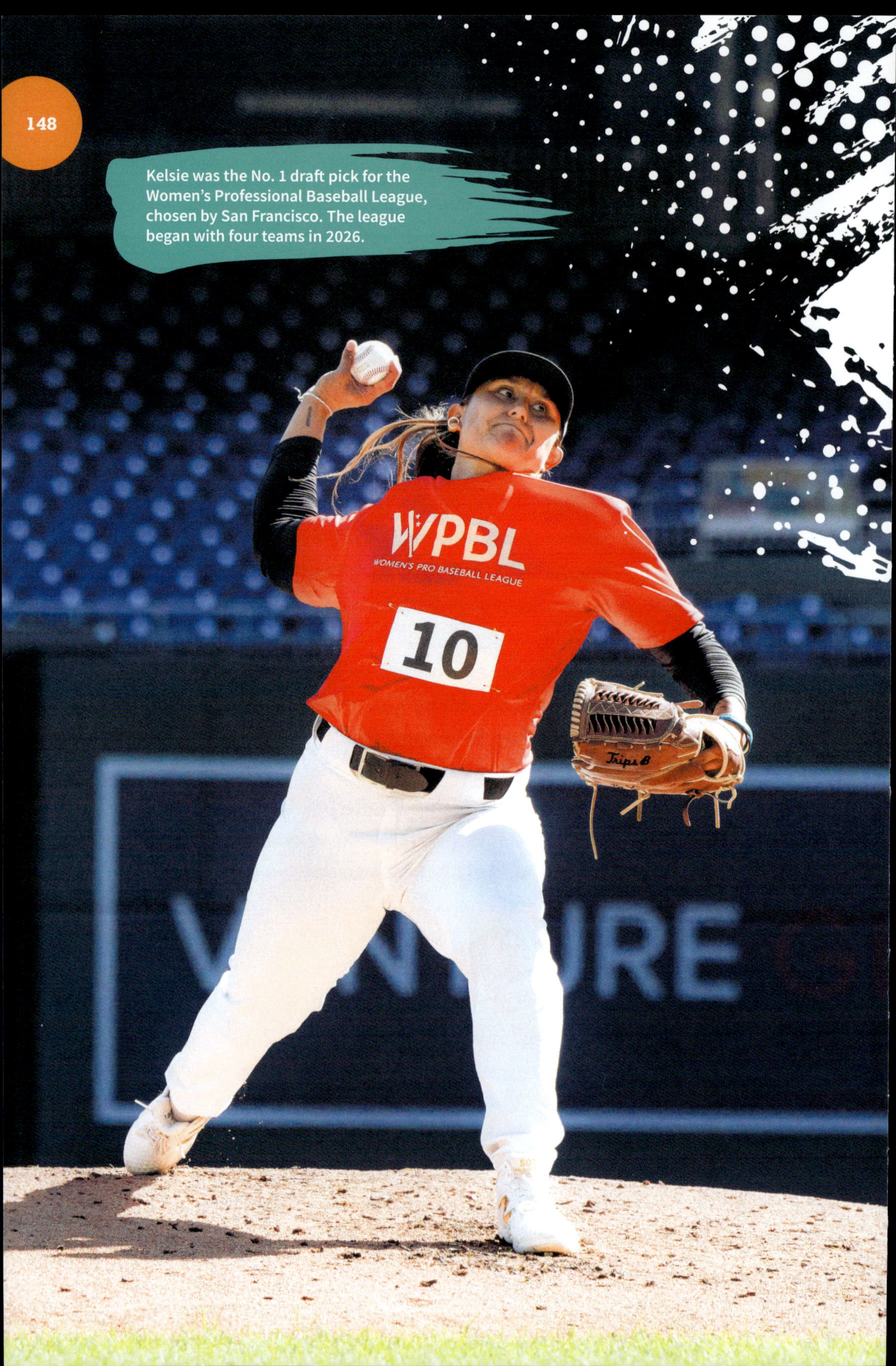

Kelsie was the No. 1 draft pick for the Women's Professional Baseball League, chosen by San Francisco. The league began with four teams in 2026.

Siegal said. "When I see her play with women, I see joy and love. And the expression of that is just one great play after another."

Kelsie is now comfortable with her role as a trailblazer. She has learned to tune out the detractors. She decided to make her messages of encouragement public by launching a clothing brand called Be You.

The hoodies say, "Chase the version of yourself you were always meant to be."

And on the back of the black T-shirt, Kelsie's affirmations read like a poem:

YOU ARE UNIQUE
YOU ARE POWERFUL
YOU ARE COURAGEOUS
YOU ARE WORTHY
YOU ARE LOVED

This is what Kelsie wants to say to teenagers today: "If you feel insecure, you feel doubtful, look yourself in the mirror. Remember who you are. You are exactly where you're supposed to be. You're there for a reason, so step up to the plate and act like it."

Amit controlled the gold medal match against Meerim Zhumanazarova of Kyrgyzstan to win, 3–0. She gave up only two points in four Olympic matches.

CHAPTER 7

AMIT ELOR, WRESTLING

"BE A PROBLEM SOLVER"

THE LINE FOR AUTOGRAPHS STRETCHES ALL THE way around the wrestling mat and nearly out the door of the gym. The 2024 United States Olympic champion Amit Elor, still in her wrestling gear, sits at a table for two hours with a gold Sharpie to make sure every girl gets what she wants. A signed poster, a selfie, a smile.

There are 93 young female wrestlers at a March 2025 clinic in Troy, New York, all there to learn from Amit, the youngest Olympic wrestling champion—male or female—in history.

For the six sweaty hours, the girls are starstruck listening to Amit teach her signature moves. At age 21, Amit has already won a gold medal and multiple world championships in dominating fashion. Her popularity is directly tied to her authentic messages of girl power, where she stands out in a space that was once only for boys.

By the end of the day, the wrestlers learn that Amit is also as sweet and strong in real life as she is on Instagram and TikTok.

"She's so pretty and she's so muscular, and that's what makes her such a great role model," says Elizabeth Bailey, 13, after reaching the front of the line. She presents Amit with a handwritten letter of admiration. Amit is so grateful, she will later post the note to social media.

"I've seen her Instagram, and she's so positive," says Maddie Hill, 15.

"Everything she posts just warms my heart, it's pure joy," adds Sophia Paone, 17.

When the line finally ends—most girls have at least three items for Amit to sign, and they all want a selfie—Amit walks out of the gym tired but happy. "I love this," she says. "Just to see how excited they were about wrestling, just melted my heart. Because growing up, people would always be like, 'Oh, you do wrestling? Like, what is that?'"

Wrestling today is one of the fastest growing sports for girls in the United States. More than 74,000 girls wrestle in high school in 46 states. When Amit won a California state high school title as a freshman in 2019, only six states allowed girls to participate in the sport and only about 20,000 girls were wrestling across the country.

Amit is quick to credit the mentors and medalists who showed her what was possible—from Helen Maroulis who won the first US women's gold in wrestling at the 2016 Rio Games to 2021 gold medalist Tamyra Mensah-Stock and 2021 silver medalist Adeline Gray. But it is clear that Amit is ushering in a new era in a sport that has always been male-dominated.

"It just seems like she's destined for greatness," US women's wrestling coach Terry Steiner said. "She just keeps winning, like losing isn't even in the conversation. It's 'how bad is she going to win?' She's this phenom that everybody has eyes on, and she continues to raise the bar."

At five-feet-seven and 158 pounds, Amit often flexes her chiseled biceps on social media to show that athletes can be both brawny and feminine. When she's not posting reels with wrestling teammates or coaches, she's posting about food, her travels, or her Israeli heritage. She has over a half-million followers on TikTok and Instagram combined.

For many Jews around the world, she is a source of pride. She sometimes posts in Hebrew (she is bilingual) and notes on days of remembrance that her grandparents were Holocaust survivors. She is careful not to delve into Israeli politics, instead posting videos about food, like making challah (braided bread) or hamantaschen (cookies for the holiday of Purim).

"It's always been a really important part of who I am, but it wasn't something that I would display to people publicly," Amit said. That has changed with her success: "Especially right now all the kinds of antisemitism going on in the world, it's something I feel I have to really be strong, no matter what kind of comments I receive."

She added quietly: "It just blows my mind. I don't understand how people can be so evil with the things they're thinking about Jewish people."

Amit is so real and honest in her social media posts. She brings her audience into her world, even to a place of vulnerability. Before winning her first Olympic gold medal, Amit had already overcome unthinkable family tragedy.

She is the youngest of six siblings born to parents who immigrated from Israel. When she was 14, her older brother, Oshry, was shot and killed in a home invasion robbery in Northern California. Four years later, Amit's father, Yair, died from complications from COVID and mental health issues.

During these terrible times, wrestling was not always a sanctuary for Amit. She was working with a coach who she said tried to motivate her using fear and negativity. The coach would often tell her that she was stupid if she didn't understand his instructions. She braced for his sudden outbursts if she did not perform in practice. He insisted his coaching method was the only way.

Amit was too afraid to complain to wrestling officials about his psychologically and verbally abusive tactics because she was so young in the sport; she still does not feel comfortable naming him.

But despite these events and perhaps also because of them, Amit learned to turn inward to find strength. When competing, she never gives her opponents an opening, instead wearing them down with her technique and her sharp instincts.

Six months after her dad died in 2022, Amit won her first world championship on the senior level. She was only 18. Then she had the courage to change coaches.

The trauma stays with her but also made her stronger.

"I'd say there's days that I feel so weak because I've been through all of this," Amit told me. "And then there's other times that I feel like life can throw anything at me and I'll come out on top."

Wrestling taught Amit Elor to be resilient.

"I can confidently say that she'll break more records," said wrestling coach Sara McMann, who trained Amit before the Paris Olympics. "If Amit stays healthy and fulfills her potential, nobody beats her until she retires."

AMIT ELOR WAS BORN ON JANUARY 1, 2004, THE year that women's wrestling debuted on the Olympic program at the Athens Games. Her family's own sports journey shaped who she is today, helping her succeed in a sport that is not typical for women.

Her father, Yair, was recruited by Boise State University in Idaho as a shot putter and a discus thrower for the track and field team in the 1980s. Her mother, Elana, had grown up playing basketball in the beach town of Ashkelon, Israel. During mandatory military training, her grip was measured to be just as strong as some men.

"I definitely got that from her," Amit said. From her dad, Amit added, "I got his strong back."

The couple settled in Walnut Creek, a suburb in the hills east of San Francisco. Elana had earned a master's degree in mechanical engineering at the University of California, Berkeley, and was working on her PhD when she gave birth to Amit. She changed careers to managing real estate properties—and to managing her children's busy sports schedules.

Sons Oshry, Orry, and Aviv played football and wrestled. The oldest child, a daughter Gilly (who is now a nuclear physicist), was a competitive fencer. The second daughter, Ronny, became the first female wrestler in the family.

Ronny, 12 years older than Amit, described herself as a big person who did not feel comfortable—or coordinated—doing gymnastics with the girls in middle school gym class. But when she saw the boys wrestle on the other side of the gym she thought: "I could definitely do that."

The gym teacher said she definitely could not. "Because you're a girl," he said.

Ronny didn't give up, joining a nearby boys' wrestling program. But when it came time to pair up with partners, no one would choose her. The only boy left would conveniently go to the bathroom and stay there. Amit would soon face the same obstacles.

Amit was four years old when she wanted to join the club where her brothers were wrestling.

"If you want to do this," her mother said, "you have to ask the coach yourself."

Amit started wrestling when she was four years old. At nine, she was already winning medals and dreaming of Olympic gold.

At the time, wrestling was not Amit's only athletic outlet. Her mom, Elana, would drop her off at the community center after school where Amit would take one class after another until evening. "I did rhythmic gymnastics, boxing, tae kwon do, judo, wrestling, jujitsu, horseback riding, swimming, tennis," Amit said. But not ball sports. She didn't like them.

Her mom took Amit to a dojo, a special judo training space, an hour south of their home every day, only stopping when that coach became ill. At first, Amit thought she wanted to become an Olympian in judo. That changed when Amit specialized in wrestling. At the ripe old age of 10.

The girls in elementary school didn't understand her passion. "Why are you rolling around on a mat with sweaty boys?" they would ask. The sweaty boys didn't exactly welcome her either. When her assigned partners would complain or avoid her, she told herself not to show any emotions.

When it came time for competing at the end of practice, Amit was ready. "The second I had the opportunity, I would use all my force and take out my anger on them," Amit said. "If they underestimated me, or if they didn't want to go with me, they would have to pay the price. That was the beating."

Unlike other combat sports, wrestling is not about contact, but about control. Wrestlers score points by placing opponents in dominating holds or by escaping from a hold, by forcing them off the mat, by grabbing and turning them, or by exposing their opponent's back to the mat. Defense turns to offense in a split-second.

"I'm not very aggressive naturally, and I don't like to hurt people," she said.

To her, wrestling is like problem solving one move at a time. Amit wrestles by what she feels from her opponent's positioning. "That's why I've never really liked ball sports, because when I wrestle, I can feel their body, and I can feel how they're moving, and I can react depending on their movements," she said.

"I like the feeling of scoring," Amit added. "It sounds simple, but I like taking people down." Especially if those people were boys. "I almost felt a sense of motivation from the fact that I was doing something that was male-dominated. It just made me even more competitive to prove to everybody, the coaches, my training partners, that I deserve to be there."

By age 11, Amit was taller and stronger than most boys or girls her age. In California, that made her different. There was only one place where she never felt self-conscious as a girl in wrestling: Israel.

Amit would spend summers with her grandparents and extended family in Ashkelon, a beach town 36 miles south of Tel Aviv. Her aunt found her a gym that offered wrestling, and Amit was finally in her element. Many of the coaches were Russian and they ran intense, demanding workouts that challenged the young wrestlers, boys and girls alike.

When she returned to California, Amit asked her mom for a Russian wrestling coach, a search that took half a year. Elana found a coach originally from Ukraine, who at first seemed to teach with the same discipline as the Russians. He worked alongside US coaches at a regional training center for USA Wrestling—only it was in Jersey City, New Jersey.

So, Elana and Amit decided that they would fly east every few months for training. But at the same time, they would seek out any gym where Amit could learn wrestling techniques. When her brother went to train at the Colorado Springs Olympic & Paralympic Training Center, she tagged along.

Since she was 12, Amit has patched together coaching

experiences to form her unique wrestling style. Life on the road came with sacrifices.

Amit took her classes online in high school through an independent study program California offered. Returning home to Northern California after weeks away, she would take all of her tests at once. Like the rest of her family, Amit excelled in math and science.

"I've never been to the high school prom and never had the full high school experience," she said. "Most of my friends were always through the wrestling world. But I wouldn't trade it because I got to have friends from all over the world, from Japan, from Russia, from Georgia, Italy, Israel."

From tournament trips with her mom where they stayed in dirty Motel 6 rooms to harrowing taxi rides in Tbilisi, Georgia, from foodie tours in Japan to synagogue visits in Budapest, mother and daughter grew even closer.

"She's my best friend," Amit said. "From the time I was five and six, I felt like we were teammates, like we were friends, and I think that's really special. I aspire to be a mom like her."

Elana was a mom and road manager, and then Amit's social media photographer, filming her daughter's TikToks. "One thing I always do is, even though I'm in the background, I always let her lead," Elana said. "I didn't want to butt in."

Elana was accompanying Amit to a tournament once in Reno, Nevada, when the unthinkable happened. During the early morning hours of April 7, 2018, Elana answered a frantic phone call from Ronny on the hotel room phone. Amit slept through the shrill ring and her mother's crying. Oshry had been murdered. He was just 23 years old. Elana kept the news from her youngest child.

In their shock, Ronny and her brother Orry drove the three hours from Walnut Creek to Reno. They needed to take care of their devastated mother, and they all decided to keep the news from Amit until after her championship match. At the time, Amit wasn't on social media.

"I woke up, and my brother and sister were in the room with me," Amit recalled. "My mom was outside on the phone. I thought it was weird."

When Amit asked, Ronny said they came to "surprise her" in the final. Amit didn't believe it.

"I kept telling Ronny, something's wrong. My mom came back, and she just smiled. She just looked fine. So, they basically hid it from me until I was done wrestling," she recalled.

For the six minutes she was on the mat, Amit blocked everything out and won. Still, in the car ride back to Walnut Creek, Elana and Ronny didn't know how to tell her.

Amit asked. "Is it my grandmother in Israel?"

She went down a list of possible events, but she couldn't fathom the worst about Oshry. "I knew he was getting in trouble. I knew bad things could happen, but the one thing that I didn't think was that he actually died," she said.

Until they told her.

Her chest clenched, "like there's no air," Amit recalled. "You can imagine something happening, right? But it's not the same as it actually happening. It's not the same as somebody telling you, 'no, this is real.'"

Oshry and Amit had had their own special bond, even though they were 10 years apart in age. He played video games with her, put her on his shoulders while hiking in the nearby hills, and they spent time in the kitchen together cooking for an imaginary restaurant they owned. Amit wrote out menus, Oshry grilled the meats. He was her protector, a sweetheart. And then he was gone.

Amit bawled in the car as her brother and sister held her.

On his gravestone, the family called Oshry a "gentle giant."

The trial took place a year later, and Amit resolved to attend every morning with her sisters. There were only a few times she needed to walk out of the courtroom because the details of the shooting, including pictures from the crime scene, were too upsetting.

The defense attorney tried to claim the shooter was acting in self-defense because Oshry, who was six-foot-five and 315 pounds, had played football and wrestled. Oshry was therefore threatening, the lawyer argued.

"Excuse me, you're going to say because somebody does wrestling, that the guy needed to act in self-defense?" Ronny said recently. "You're attacking us as a family now because he's big and he wrestled?"

The jury convicted the shooter, and the sentencing happened just as the world shut down for COVID.

After Oshry's death and then the start of the pandemic, Amit's father, Yair Elor, had started to isolate himself, living in one of the houses the family owned and rented. Elana and her children did not know how to help him. He became obsessed with conspiracy theories about COVID, Elana and Orry said.

On April 10, 2022, Amit and Elana were in Jersey City at the New Jersey Regional Training Center when they got the news that Yair had passed away. Again, they returned for a family funeral and a week of mourning in the Jewish tradition. His gravestone is next to Oshry's.

"If there was one thing that my dad was, he was just very, very proud of all of us equally. And he was a blubber mouth," Amit said. "I would be going to a local gas station or something, and they would go, 'are you the daughter of that guy who always talks about his kids? Oh, so you're the

As a teen, Amit would always be atop the podium, including the 2016 national boys' folkstyle championship.

wrestler, aren't you? You beat up all the boys. Oh yeah, he told me about you.' "

By the time Amit was 16, Yair was telling everybody: "She's going to win the Olympics."

Four years later, he was right.

"I know he really believed in me," Amit said. "I wish he could have had the joy of witnessing it."

- - - - ★ - - - -

AMIT CAME INTO HER FIRST OLYMPICS HAVING won six championships at her age levels and two on the senior level. She had not lost a match since 2019, dominating international competition because of her unique style. Amit immediately puts herself in a controlling position, like grabbing an opponent's arm with two hands, and forcing her opponent to make mistakes.

"Aggressive defense," is how Steiner, the national team coach, described her tactics.

"It's not a sexy style of wrestling, high-flying and a lot of points," he said. "How do you win a lot of matches? You don't get scored on. She's very patient with her positioning."

Amit's tactics, in part, come from watching her brother Orry compete in Greco-Roman wrestling, where wrestlers can only use their upper bodies to take down an opponent. Orry wrestled in college and finished fourth in the 2016 Olympics trials. Although women only compete in freestyle wrestling in the Olympics—where they can score points by using both their upper and lower body—Amit's emphasis on upper body moves gives her an edge.

Amit missed the age cutoff to compete in the COVID-delayed 2021 Tokyo Olympics by one day. She had to be 17 on December 31, 2020. She turned 17 the following day.

When it came time to train for Paris in 2024, her coaches decided she would wrestle in the 68-kilogram (149.5 pounds) weight class, nine pounds lighter than where she wrestled for world championships. (That was necessary because at the time, the Olympics only had six classifications for men and women while the world championships had 10.)

Amit's journey to gold got off to a bad start. She couldn't find her lucky bracelet in her bedroom and nearly missed her flight because she didn't want to leave home without it. She would find the bracelet at home months later between a stack of clothes. On the flight from San Francisco to Paris, Amit got very sick. She couldn't stop coughing and contracted a high fever.

By the time she recovered, she had lost strength and only had time for two practices. But that didn't matter—she'd had a lifetime of preparation.

To avoid the distraction of staying with other Olympians in the Olympic Village, Amit instead stayed in an apartment her family rented. Orry interrupted his PhD program in pharmaceutical science to become his sister's full-time chef and nutritionist leading up to her matches. He figured out down to the exact calorie how much fat, protein, and carbohydrates she needed to fuel herself. (She had a piece of a famous French baguette only once.)

Even with her mom and sister Ronny encouraging her, Amit was still uncharacteristically nervous before her first match.

Her coach, Sara McMann, who had won a silver medal at the 2004 Olympics, had an idea of how to calm her down. When they arrived at the arena an hour before warm-ups, McMann sweetly asked the volunteers if she could bring Amit onto the floor so she could see where she would soon compete. Envisioning the space relaxed Amit.

She told herself: "There are three mats on the floor, just like every other big tournament. Two periods, each three minutes. One opponent at a time. I can do this."

On paper, her first match seemed to be the toughest. And yet, when Amit met the defending world champion and top-seeded wrestler from Turkey in Round 1, she dominated her, winning 10–2. Amit conceded those two points in the final 10 seconds when the match was essentially over. They were the only two points Amit gave up all Olympics.

In the quarterfinals, Amit won, 8–0. In her semifinal bout against the defending Olympic champion from Korea, she won in 1 minute, 45 seconds by technical superiority: as soon as she scored the first 10 points, the match was over.

All three early-round matches occurred on her father's birthday, making her success that much more special, but bittersweet.

For the final on the next day, the match was typical Amit: low scoring and controlling with technique. Her 3–0 triumph was never in question.

After the referee raised Amit's hand to signal her victory, Amit flexed her left biceps and draped the American flag on her shoulders, running circles around the mat. Then she raced to the side of the stands where her family sat and formed the heart sign with her fingers.

The ultimate flex: Amit celebrated in 2024 after becoming the youngest US wrestler (female or male) to win an Olympic gold medal.

Through tears, she told the NBC cameras: "Anything hard in life, unfortunately, makes you stronger and I think I am able to carry myself the way I am because of the hardships I've been through."

LOOKING AHEAD TO THE LOS ANGELES OLYMPICS IN 2028, Amit is encouraged by the talent of women's wrestling in the United States. Still, she wants more: more weight classes for women on the international level. Better locker room and workout facilities for women in traditional male spaces like the New York Athletic Club. She still sees inequity in media coverage of men's and women's wrestling and is dismayed when she hears that men think they should earn more than women.

Amit wants to get to the point where "you see a female wrestler, and she's not a 'woman wrestler,'" she said. "She's just a wrestler."

In 2025, she signed a contract with Nike, and they began developing her own logo, a silhouette of her in a wrestling singlet, flexing her biceps—Amit's signature pose.

For female or male wrestlers, there aren't many post-Olympic options to make money in the sport. Mixed martial arts (MMA) incorporates boxing, judo, and wrestling, but emphasizes fighting as part of a show. World Wrestling Entertainment (WWE), where the former Olympic champion Tamyra Mensah-Stock is working, is mostly staged and wrestlers must play their roles. For women, that means dressing provocatively for a young male audience and talking trash to their opponents.

"That's just not who she is," McMann said. "She'll figure

out the ways to get money in the ways that suit her. She likes to do entertainment on her own terms."

Amit said she is not at all interested in joining WWE or competing in MMA.

"It's frustrating, but I want to make wrestling popular enough that girls can be like, all I want to do is wrestle, and I will be successful with this, and I'll make a name for myself just through wrestling," Amit said.

For now, Amit earns a yearly stipend (less than $50,000) from the national organization that oversees the Olympic and world championship teams—USA Wrestling. In exchange for training facilities and travel expenses, Amit runs about four wrestling clinics a year. In the summer of 2025, she ran some 15 clinics, which her mom and sister helped manage.

In September 2025, Amit announced why she was teaching and not competing: she was expecting a baby with her long-time boyfriend from Brazil, Mica Galvão, a professional jujitsu fighter. The two had gotten engaged and later moved to Southern California to start their new life.

Amit trained throughout her pregnancy, documenting it on social media. On January 23, 2026, she gave birth to Aryeh Elor Galvão, who weighed in at 8 pounds, 2 ounces, and 21 inches. In Hebrew, Aryeh means "lion."

"I've always wanted to be a mom, but I thought it would have to wait until I retire from wrestling. I'm so blessed to live this dream of starting a family, and so grateful my baby will be with me on my journey to the LA 2028 Olympics," she wrote on Instagram.

She was glowing on and off social media, embracing this new challenge in her life. "I've kind of always done things my own way," Amit told me. "And I've really learned that you don't have to do exactly what somebody else does to reach success."

In each of her clinics, Amit always reserves an hour or more for a Q&A session where the students sit on the mat and ask questions. The clinic in Troy was no different. She offered actionable advice for young wrestlers:

WHAT IS YOUR NUTRITION ADVICE?

"I used to be obsessed with protein, like having a Greek yogurt and eggs. Now that I have more experience competing and have had sports nutritionists, I eat mostly carbs and, of course, some water with electrolytes. It obviously depends how much weight you cut, but if you feel like you're even slightly dehydrated, that can put your muscles at risk, you can get injured more easily, and that decreases performance. So, hydration is really important, and then eating things that your body can absorb and digest really quickly. So, for me, that's really simple, fast digesting carbs, like honey and white bread."

"What matters is that you're happy with yourself."

WHAT IS YOUR PRE-MATCH ROUTINE?

"I make sure to study all my opponents. I visualize myself wrestling this person. Five minutes before, I'm envisioning myself wrestling them in my head. And if it gets to be too much, I'll just stop and distract myself. It's about this constant balance of being in the moment."

HOW DO YOU STAY MOTIVATED?

"What wrestling taught me at a young age was being able to ignore how I felt mentally and physically to perform anyway. There's times that you feel so beat up because you feel so tired and you wrestle anyways, and there's also times that you feel very hurt mentally, you feel broken down, you feel sad, you feel angry, all sorts of feelings that wrestling can bring up, and you still have to put that to the side and wrestle anyone. So those are things that wrestling teaches you, which I think are super valuable for all areas of life."

She added that kids should not be afraid to ask for help. "Do I need to talk to somebody about how I'm feeling right now, instead of just constantly ignoring my emotions? It's important to recognize what's going on mentally, and if you need to talk to someone."

HOW ARE YOU SO CONFIDENT? AND HOW DO YOU RESPOND TO DOUBTERS?

"Even if you don't believe you can do it, tell yourself you can. I have this drive in me to prove that they're wrong and also to prove to myself, and my community. At the end of the day, people are going to have their opinions. What matters is that you're happy with yourself."

When McKenzie was a baby, doctors thought she might never walk. She has won seven Paralympic medals, and is training for more.

CHAPTER 8

McKENZIE COAN, SWIMMING

"CELEBRATE OUR DIFFERENCES"

HER SWEET SIXTEEN WAS OFF TO A SAD START. McKenzie Coan had traveled from her home in Georgia to Bismarck, North Dakota, to try to qualify for the 2012 London Paralympics. Now, on her milestone birthday, she was watching the water drain from her dream.

At the morning preliminary for the 400-meter freestyle race—her best event—McKenzie swam the worst eight laps of her young career.

She felt as if the relentless cycle of broken bones, surgeries, body casts, torturous rehabilitation, and rigorous training she endured as an elite athlete born with osteogenesis imperfecta (OI)—a rare disability that makes bones brittle—would be in vain.

McKenzie returned to her hotel room, told her mom to leave, turned off the lights, queued Rihanna, Britney, and Taylor, and reminded herself why she started swimming: *to be free*.

In the pool, all the pressure on her bones disappeared. Now she somehow had to shake off the heavy weight of her own expectations.

A few hours later, McKenzie returned to the pool for the 400-meter final to qualify for her first Paralympics. "It's just water," Teresa Coan, her mother and coach, told her, trying to cut the tension.

McKenzie swam her fastest 400 meters ever. She was going to London.

That 16th birthday performance would be a gift McKenzie would return to whenever she needed a reminder of her ability rather than her disability. The seven Paralympic medals she would go on to win were her other reminders.

No one knows why McKenzie was born with this terrible genetic disorder. She has broken more than 100 bones—she lost count years ago. OI usually brings associated conditions, including scoliosis, dwarfism, and respiratory restrictions. McKenzie has them all. The dangers are plenty for a nonathlete. A sneeze could break a rib. Just slipping on a floor wearing socks could (and did) put McKenzie in a cast.

For an elite athlete with OI, the risks are magnified. Even in the pool McKenzie is not immune. She has broken fingers, toes, ankles, and ribs from flip turns or from arching her back.

Doctors diagnosed McKenzie's condition when she was 19 days old; Teresa had heard a pop when she was burping her. McKenzie, unusually tiny and bowlegged, had a broken leg. An X-ray revealed she had first broken it when she was in her mother's womb. The disorder affects a small population of babies in the US; infants with recognizable OI at birth make up about one in every 16,000 to 20,000 births. Her father, Marc Coan, is an internist who had never treated a child with OI.

At the time, the doctors said McKenzie might not sit up, walk, or even live past infancy. They saw her body, not her determined soul.

When McKenzie was six months old, her physical therapist, Colleen O'Berry, issued a challenge to Teresa that would define McKenzie's life:

"You have two choices. She can be a china doll in a cabinet, or you can let her live."

O'Berry added a caveat: "And when she lives, she's going to have fractures. But so does every other child. People get hurt, people get sick. It's no different."

But in the small town of Clarkesville, Georgia (population 2,135), two hours northeast of Atlanta, McKenzie *was* different. She was the only kid in a bright pink wheelchair. People didn't know how to act around her or what to say to her. When they did say something, it wasn't always nice. McKenzie and her family did their best to respond thoughtfully.

"I've always felt as an athlete with a disability, and as a person with a disability. . . I have to give a little extra to educate people," she told me, adding that she'd remain calm even when people acted insensitively.

She continued, "If they had a positive experience with me, showing them that I can do something, maybe they won't do that same thing to somebody else who looks like me or who gets around like me."

Of course, to one teenage boy who asked her why her body was "like that," McKenzie responded with sass: "I didn't eat my vegetables."

Some people are not worth educating. And that's their loss.

McKenzie is a joyful, engaging, smart, sensitive, silly, and fierce woman. She's the friend you want to talk deep into the night with about fixing the world or about the latest bestseller or about *Legally Blonde*, her favorite childhood movie. She is a gifted storyteller, and she genuinely wants to connect with you.

But play a game of Ping-Pong, charades, or UNO and she will try to beat you to a pulp. Her parents actually banned Monopoly in the house because things got too heated with her brothers. Let's just say McKenzie is fiercely competitive.

McKenzie is no different than any other elite athlete. She is a perfectionist. It's as if she is trying to erase the "imperfecta" part of the name of her disability.

Whatever McKenzie can control, she does to the greatest degree—especially her swim bag. Everything has its place. Goggles and cap in the inside zipper pocket, with a spare cap and goggles in a separate small bag in that pocket.

"I cannot function if they're not back in that pocket," she said. "It doesn't matter if I've been out of the water for 30 seconds, I need them to be back in that same specific spot."

McKenzie added: "My towel has to be rolled in a very specific way. I can't hold it. It has to be rolled because that's how everything slides in properly. And that's especially true if you have two towels, so they go in rolled on the outside compartment of the swim bag."

The water bottle goes in one spot for competitions (outside pocket), another place for practice (inside). In another, outside pocket she puts her headphones, followed by her tempo trainer for laps, Band-Aids, and a mini first-aid kit. Below that outside pocket, she puts her suits. Those that are still wet go in a special bag within that pocket, of course.

The swim bag gives McKenzie control because when you're competing, she said, "there's such a sense of the 'uncontrollables' that surround you."

Those "uncontrollables" carry over to her condition.

"I never had a choice when I would fracture a bone; I never had a choice about how bad it was going to hurt," she said. "The only thing I had a choice in was my outlook and how I got through it. So, I think that really has actually carried over into every other part of my life."

In many ways, the rigorous routine of swimming and the weightlessness of the water have allowed her to forget about her fragile bones. Her success has given her some measure of control over an unpredictable life.

"Celebrate our differences" is what I say to those who have trouble seeing past wheelchairs or labels. In my lifelong fight for equity and inclusiveness, I have long been an advocate for para sports (from the Greek term for side-by-side) that allow elite athletes with disabilities to participate. Sometimes they need equipment modifications—like in wheelchair tennis—and other times they can train alongside able-bodied athletes but participate in distinct classifications—as in para swimming.

I was thrilled to see how the 2024 Paris Paralympics brought attention to elite athletes with a range of disabilities. Those games were the best-attended since 2012 and the most-watched ever, with 763.3 million hours of live coverage consumed globally. All the athletes in Paris could feel the energy.

"It finally feels like the world is paying attention for all the right reasons," McKenzie said. "Yes, it's really incredible that we go out there as athletes with disabilities and compete on this level. But I want to inspire you, not because I get out of bed every day and somehow make it to a pool, but because I'm an elite athlete who just so happens to have a disability."

TO UNDERSTAND McKENZIE, YOU HAVE TO understand her high-achieving, no-nonsense, self-assured family. Teresa, a proud native of Chattanooga, Tennessee, taught McKenzie and her brothers Grant and Eli to be confident and to embrace one cardinal rule: be kind.

"There's always someone worse off than you," Teresa would tell them.

Teresa learned early to suppress her own fear of McKenzie getting hurt or worse so that her daughter would not panic. She had McKenzie's older brother, Grant, even help with her care when he was still a toddler.

He was just two-and-a-half years old when he learned to take Popsicles from the freezer so that Teresa could make a splint whenever baby McKenzie broke a bone, which was often. It's no wonder that Grant is a physician today.

Eli was born 18 months after McKenzie. Like his brother, he is able-bodied. He and McKenzie have always been besties, their playful, adventurous personalities joined. He is a pilot and a swim coach today.

At age five, McKenzie went in for a surgery that required a full body cast for her barely three-foot-tall frame. Doctors asked what color she wanted for her cast. She replied: "Pink with a chrome sparkle."

Her surgery lasted three hours longer than it should have, causing her parents to think something awful had happened. The medical staff just needed the extra time to mix two kinds of paint.

"I knew what I wanted," McKenzie said, laughing.

When the cast came off six weeks later, McKenzie returned to physical therapy. At the time, she was doing aqua therapy in a baby pool, wearing a protective vest, while her brothers were swimming in the regulation pool at the same complex. She was a bit envious of Grant and Eli.

McKenzie told her mother she wanted to join their team, the Habersham Rapids. The coach said she would have to swim one lap first like the other kids trying out: 25 yards.

McKenzie had never been in the water without a life jacket. After her mother tossed it in the garbage can, McKenzie walked into the big pool and soon she found herself underwater. To this day she can still see the bubbles rising above her. She was not about to let herself sink. She rose up and swam a lap. It felt amazing. Then another. Then another. She swam—more like paddled at that point—six laps just to prove that she could.

McKenzie loved being silly and having fun on the pool deck but was fiercely competitive in the water.

"That feeling of freedom that I felt in the aqua therapy pool was just amplified by 100," McKenzie recalled. "I was all alone, and it was up to me. That's the part I really loved, because so many people underestimated what I was capable of on land."

Within two years, McKenzie improved dramatically. She was one of the top swimmers in her age group. She was not quite four feet tall, but her coach nicknamed her "Big Mac."

At eight years old, McKenzie won her first big race, beating an able-bodied swimmer. The other girl bawled, saying that she had lost to "someone in a wheelchair."

She did not have a wheelchair in the water.

McKenzie would hear snide comments from the pool decks and the stands. Officials thought she should not be swimming the same distances. Parents who did not like to see their children lose to a disabled athlete would give her the side-eye and shake their heads disapprovingly.

"That's just the most satisfying thing in the world to me to think about when I'm at a Games, whether I'm standing there on the podium or I'm in the warm-up pool, just simply taking in the fact that I'm there and, and guess who's not here," McKenzie said with a broad smile.

"They will never know this level that I've reached, and some of it was because of their words," she said, adding, "Because even through the disappointments that I faced, the injuries that I was going through, I was never going to let them win. I was not going to let them have that kind of negative power over me to where I second guess myself—'well, maybe they're right?' There was never a question of that."

The Coan kids were all motivated and disciplined. They would get up at 5 a.m., eat breakfast, drive to the pool, swim from 6 to 7:30, return home and split into different rooms for school. They each had their own desks all over the house. At noon, they would regroup with their mom to go over their assignments. They would compare outcomes, still competing.

After dinner, Teresa would go to her job as a respiratory therapist, working the night shift. She slept about three hours, recalling her days as a college student when she worked full-time at a hospital at night to pay for her classes during the day. "I was never afraid of hard work," she said.

Teresa and Marc raised McKenzie to do everything her two brothers did, only in an adapted way. She wanted to ride a horse? Her parents found a horse who also had OI. She wanted to skateboard? Her parents tied a rope to the end of the board and pulled her around the driveway on it.

Whenever people asked why Teresa would put her daughter at so-called "risk" by doing such activities, she would tell them: "Why in the world would you try to stop her? Why would you try to limit her? I always see her for what she can do, and I would hope that you do the same thing."

McKenzie once played a fierce game of Ping-Pong in her wheelchair against her mother on a Girl Scout trip. "What is WRONG with you?" an adult chaperone, the mother of another Girl Scout, shouted at McKenzie for competing too hard.

Teresa put down her paddle and put down the ball.

"I looked at McKenzie, and I kind of did my Tennessee laugh. And I went, 'I don't see anything wrong with her.'" Teresa recalled.

She turned to McKenzie and said, "Anything wrong with you?"

"Nope," McKenzie answered.

"I don't think so either," Teresa said. And mother and daughter left the room.

Teresa reminded McKenzie that there was nothing wrong with her when she went into the hospital for intravenous (IV) infusions to increase her bone density every three months. They made McKenzie sick to her stomach and feverish. Still, Teresa pointed out that she was not sick like other children in the hospital.

They devised a routine. Each time McKenzie was admitted for the infusions, usually for a week, they would throw a party for the other children on the floor.

"There's kids that are less fortunate in this hospital than you, and it's your job to bring joy to others," Teresa told her. McKenzie and her brothers constructed elaborate figures out of colored craft noodles for cancer patients to play with. One time, they took a snowball machine into the hospital; another time they gave out coloring sets.

"We never felt sorry for ourselves," Teresa said. "We always felt blessed."

AROUND THE TIME McKENZIE WAS 11, SHE REALIZED she could compete on a team with other para swimmers. While still training with the Habersham Rapids, McKenzie also joined a regional para team that practiced once a week. That put her on course to compete in national para swim meets.

McKenzie tried out for the 2008 US Paralympics swim team and finished fifth in the 400 meters. Teresa thought she could go farther if she had a more competitive training experience. Her brothers were also improving, and Teresa enrolled all three swimming siblings in a new program with an intense coach.

This coach was not only demanding in his workouts, McKenzie recalled he also did not treat her fairly as the only para swimmer. She would consistently finish drills last, and he made the rest of the team swim extra laps because of it. Then he dropped Grant, a long-distance specialist who would go on to swim competitively in college, to a second-tier group.

Grant, then 13, felt the coach was discriminating against his sister. He told the coach that the family would be leaving the program.

And that was the beginning of the era of Teresa coaching the Coan children. McKenzie took to calling her, "Moach." In the morning, Teresa would supervise McKenzie's workouts at the Frances Meadows Aquatic Center in Gainesville, Georgia, near their house. Then she supervised McKenzie's and Eli's schooling. By that point, Grant was attending Rabun Gap-Nacoochee School, a private high school an hour away. Teresa was the swim coach there, too. Rather than leave McKenzie at home, she brought her and Eli to the pool for Grant's practice.

Eli sat in the stands, but McKenzie got into the pool to do an extra practice with Grant's team. "She had this mindset that, 'Hey, I'm sitting here. I might as well get another four or 5,000 yards a day in,'" Grant recalled.

The children spent a lot of time in the family minivan—her mother wearing out one car after another. They had two red minivans, a purple one, and a blue one—followed by a Ford Explorer and a GMC Yukon that finally died with 400,000 miles on it. On the long drives on Georgia highways, McKenzie sometimes rewatched *Legally Blonde* in the back seat.

McKenzie saw herself as Reese Witherspoon's iconic Elle Woods character; she, too, was always underestimated. She, too, loved pink. And just like Elle, McKenzie wanted to be a lawyer even at age 12.

She first started watching the movie after a life-threatening surgery to replace the supporting rods in her legs. That surgery left her in yet another body cast at age 12. When she returned from the hospital after being in the intensive care unit (she had lost a lot of blood during the procedure), Teresa allowed McKenzie to mope. She let her feel the pain—but only for 48 hours.

"I knew if I had let it consume me, that would be the end of it, that that would be the end of everything," McKenzie said. "That would be the end of my motivation, that would be the end of my optimism. It would just destroy my life and my family's in so many different ways. So, I knew I just had 48 hours to feel it, but then from that point on, you can't sulk anymore."

MANY ELITE ATHLETES CITE THEIR EARLY interactions with stars of the sport as formative moments. McKenzie had two very different takeaways from these meetings.

She recalled how an able-bodied swimmer, an Olympic medalist, came to visit her swim team in Georgia one day. The swimmer showed off two medals in a box on a table. (McKenzie did not want to share the athlete's name because she did not want to shame them.) When McKenzie and a few other swimmers peered over the table, the Olympian barked: "Back up, you're breathing on the medals!"

McKenzie was horrified. She said to herself: "If I'm ever lucky enough to win a medal one day, I want to share it with people. I want them to see it and hold it and know that this is something within their reach."

Today, she keeps her medals in socks she purchased at Walmart. They are scratched, chipped, and fingerprinted—especially around the words in Braille, which all Paralympic medals feature. "These get loved on quite a bit," McKenzie said.

When she was 14, McKenzie was able to meet Kara Ayers, a US Paralympic swimmer who also had OI. Ayers was eight months pregnant when she came to a meet near her home in Cincinnati to watch McKenzie swim for three hours. So captivated by McKenzie's performance and her personality, Ayers joined Teresa and McKenzie for dinner. Her body and McKenzie's looked similar: curved spines, bowed bones, short stature. The two swimmers bonded.

"I think you at times feel alone as a para swimmer, period, no matter what our disability, because the vast majority of us train and practice either on our own or with teams that we're the only para athlete, or the only athlete with OI," Ayers said.

Ayers could relate to the frustration McKenzie had over the subjective classification system for international swim meets. Para swimming's classification system considers athletes who have varying degrees of disabilities in three categories: physical disabilities, intellectual disabilities, and vision impairment. There are rules to prevent athletes from lying about the severity of their disability to get a more favorable classification.

But because some athletes' conditions tend to worsen when they get older, classification systems can change. And when they change before a scheduled competition, that affects everybody else's ranking in the same event. Since McKenzie can walk without a wheelchair, she started as an S8. (The higher the number, the lesser the disability.) As her condition worsened, she became an S7.

Classification assessments take place usually six weeks before an international meet.

This can cause a shake-up in the events after each country's trials. At the 2012 London Games, a swimmer with faster times was reclassified into McKenzie's division, which bumped McKenzie from two other events for which she had originally qualified.

When McKenzie left London, she planned for a future on the medal stand. She became even more independent. She got her driver's license for a vehicle adapted to her. She left home for Loyola University Maryland, whose coach, Brian Loeffler, had been on the US Paralympic staff.

For McKenzie, leaving Georgia felt like she was shedding her life jacket once again. Her dad was no longer there to leave the porch light on so she could walk from the car to the front door. Her mom could only encourage her by phone.

At Loyola, McKenzie joined other aspiring Paralympic swimmers as they competed alongside able-bodied swimmers in collegiate competition. They also trained twice a week as a group for the 2016 Rio Paralympics. McKenzie felt ready—at least until she suffered an injury at the team training camp two weeks before those Paralympics.

While practicing backstroke sets, McKenzie arched her back a bit too far and fractured a rib. She heard the telltale pop and felt the pain instantly. She told her coaches she was fine. But after one terrible practice in which her coach yelled at her for slow reactions (not knowing why), McKenzie went to a mat behind the pool, lay on her stomach, and bawled. She called her mother.

Teresa told McKenzie how strong she was to endure this latest break. She texted pictures of McKenzie swimming as a child, McKenzie playing as a toddler. "She's counting on you," Teresa said of McKenzie's past self.

McKenzie was determined not to let any version of herself down. The water calmed her nerves, and the adrenaline masked her pain. When she got to Rio for the

Mackenzie and her mom, Teresa, at the 2016 Rio Paralympic Games. A few hours after she broke the American record in the preliminary heat of the 50-meter freestyle, S7 McKenzie won her first gold medal.

2016 Paralympics, she made the final of the 100-meter backstroke, which served as a warm-up to the freestyle events.

Day Three was the 50-meter freestyle, a sprint. McKenzie wasn't expecting too much because she considered herself more of a distance specialist. McKenzie swam the race of her life, breaking the then-Paralympic record of 32.42 seconds. She had just won her first gold medal.

She didn't realize that people would rush to see this precious shiny symbol of excellence and swarm her with congratulations. For someone who cautiously navigated crowds, this was unnerving. She walked into the stands escorted by a Department of Homeland Security guard. Her younger brother, Eli, did the rest, blocking fans from crowding her.

Suddenly, McKenzie saw a girl sitting in a pink wheelchair on the landing, a girl with the same telltale body type of OI. It turned out she and her mother had traveled hours from a small town in Brazil just to see McKenzie swim.

"I took my medal off and put it around her because that's what the moment is all about," McKenzie said. "Winning gold medals and breaking records, all that is really fun. But I realize the impact is much bigger than winning shiny things and having something to show off."

Nearby, her mother was crying. "That's the moment she made it, in my eyes," Teresa said.

McKenzie won two more gold medals—in the 100-meter and 400-meter freestyle. She was chosen to swim the leadoff leg in the 400-meter freestyle relay for her team and won silver.

But that wasn't the only memory from this incredible summer. In the lead-up to Rio, McKenzie read biographies of athletes to motivate her. She was obsessed with the gymnast Shawn Johnson's book, *Winning Balance*, about the 2008 Beijing Olympics where Johnson won the all-around gold medal.

"There's a part where she talked about her experience in Beijing in 2008 with one of the other athletes, he was a cyclist," McKenzie said. They had their first kiss. "It's just the cutest thing ever. It's absolutely adorable."

McKenzie would have her own adorable story in Rio. A brown-haired, US para soccer player spotted her early in the village while she was in the middle of competition and tried to make small talk. She didn't really listen to him. A few days later, he brought her a churro with chocolate and caramel dipping sauces. She insisted she couldn't eat while in the middle of competing, but she nibbled the ends to be a good sport. But he was persistent and patient.

At the closing ceremony, the soccer player (she didn't want to give his name) joined her group of athletes who left early. He had a plan: he brought a beanbag and invited her to the roof. They cuddled and gazed at the stars—until McKenzie was utterly embarrassed to see her swim coaches walk by. The roof was public. They scrunched down deeper in the beanbag chair, and he kissed her sweetly.

McKenzie still smiles when thinking about that rooftop night. "He was a really, really nice person. It was kind of cool to have an almost normal experience, since I didn't have that in high school," she said.

When she returned with three gold medals, a silver, and a swoony memory of a kiss, McKenzie did not have time to float in the glory. She had a rib that needed healing. Adidas signed her as a sponsored athlete and sent her to speaking engagements. She got to throw out the first pitch at a Baltimore Orioles game. She shook President Obama's hand in a White House ceremony to celebrate the Paralympians.

In 2018, McKenzie celebrated senior day at the University of Loyola Maryland with her parents and Brian Loeffler (left), the head coach of Loyola Maryland Swimming and Diving.

"Winning gold medals and breaking records, all that is really fun. But I realize the impact is much bigger than winning shiny things and having something to show off."

She also had to return to Loyola and make up three weeks of missed classes. Life was surreal and all too real at the same time.

McKenzie graduated Loyola in 2018 with a degree in political science and was named to the academic honor roll.

NEXT UP FOR McKENZIE WAS THE 2020 TOKYO Paralympics. But athletes had an unexpected disruption when COVID hit. Marc and Teresa, ever the dedicated parents, built a resistance pool for McKenzie in their garage. But that 15-foot pool was not nearly the same distance as a 50-meter Olympic pool, and McKenzie needed more than a simulated experience.

When the Games were postponed until 2021, McKenzie lived in a COVID-safe bubble at the Colorado Springs Olympic & Paralympic Training Center. That isolation paid off when McKenzie won a gold and a silver medal in a Tokyo Paralympics that had no fans.

After winning medals at two straight Paralympics, McKenzie thought she was ready to pursue her post-athletic dreams. She started at Rutgers Law School and loved her classes. And yet, the pool was still calling her. For the first time, there would be a meet that brought Paralympic and Olympic swimmers together on the same team, competing against Australia. She withdrew from law school, confident she could apply again when the time was right.

The 2022 Duel in the Pool was held in Sydney, Australia, and McKenzie had a blast. She won the mixed multi-class 100-meter freestyle event. She would be ready for the 2024 Olympics. Or so she thought.

No matter how much athletes plan, injuries can happen at the worst times. McKenzie had learned at a young age how

After winning a silver medal in the 100-meter freestyle, S7 race at the Tokyo Olympics in 2021, McKenzie offered congratulations to bronze medalist, Yelyzaveta Mereshko of Ukraine. McKenzie had also won gold in the 400-meter free.

to deal with pain and uncertainty, but she would experience the hardest year of her career in 2023. One day, she woke up with Bell's palsy, a sudden paralysis that not only affected her facial muscles, but also the hearing in her left ear and the muscles on the left side of her upper body. She could not breathe fully. She could not swim.

Whenever she had any surgery, she always had a strict timetable for recovery. For the first time in her life, McKenzie couldn't even follow her mom's rule. She found herself depressed for more than 48 hours.

There were days when she neither felt physically nor mentally able to get out of bed. At the beginning of 2024, doctors delivered more bad news: they thought she might have cancer. What more could she endure?

After further tests a few weeks later, McKenzie learned she did not have cancer. Her Bell's palsy finally subsided by April. McKenzie had just three months to prepare for the 2024 US Paralympic Team Trials in Minneapolis in June.

When she got there, it was like 2012 all over again. She had a horrible preliminary swim in her best event, the 400-meter freestyle.

"I'm sitting there, and I'm like, I cannot let this one moment define me," McKenzie recalled. "I didn't do it back then. There's no reason I'm going to do it now. I just have to go out there and do what I know I'm capable of."

She went back to her hotel. Shut the door. Queued Rihanna and Britney and cleared her mind. McKenzie, like all champions, came through in the clutch. She made her fourth Paralympic team.

"I hadn't swum that fast or really executed in that way in probably over a year," she said. "Just making it to the games was a huge accomplishment."

It was on to Paris. McKenzie relied on muscle memory to swim her favorite and best event. As soon as she dove into the pool, she knew she would medal in the 400 meters. Her strategy—saving her strength for the final 200 meters—paid off. With 35 meters left on the last lap, and a narrow lead on an Italian swimmer, McKenzie felt like she did in Rio eight years earlier.

Her teammate, Morgan Stickney, was already at the wall to win the gold medal. McKenzie finished second and burst into happy tears.

"I just knew everything had come together as perfectly as it could have in that moment. . . . Everything that I had been through was worth it, but more so everything I've been through in my life to get there was also worth it," she recalled.

"I look down at my silver, and to me it feels like gold," she added.

As she has grown older, McKenzie has redefined her concept of success: "It's maturity as an athlete, realizing that every time you dive in, it may not be gold, but was the performance there? Was the execution there? Did you represent your country to the absolute best of your ability?"

The answer was "yes," to all those questions.

Paris was her fourth Paralympic games and, when her program ended, she finally felt like she could let loose while watching other events. Her boyfriend, Micah, came along with her family to support her. She made sure to enjoy every moment from both the opening and closing ceremonies.

And yet, part of her was a bit disappointed. The media coverage for the Paralympians had been tiny compared to the Olympic athletes. Inequity, in training support and in athlete stipends, always existed between the able-boded Team USA athletes and Paralympians. And this was true even after the governing body changed its name to the United States Olympic and Paralympic Committee in 2019. The USOPC.

"Yeah, they have the 'P,' but sometimes it seems like it's just there for looks," McKenzie said, having spent more than two years as a member of the athlete's advisory group.

Olympians and Paralympians earn the same prize money for their medals, a change made for Tokyo in 2021. But training the next generation of Paralympic athletes is not a priority, McKenzie said, like it is in Olympic sports. For example, she noted that US Para Swimming cut the full-time training program in Colorado Springs in October 2024.

"I'll be back one day, and I won't be a competing athlete anymore, and I will have a law degree," McKenzie said, "and I can promise you that things are not going to be the status quo, because I don't want other athletes going through what I've been through."

McKenzie is planning to practice civil rights and disability law, and in fall 2025 started a master's program in policy. This will prepare her for law school, which she now plans to attend after the Los Angeles Paralympics in 2028. For her, finishing her career on home turf represents more than just a competitive opportunity.

"It shows an entire generation sitting at home with a disability that they're worthy, and they're capable of doing really great things," she said.

"It's more important than ever now," McKenzie said, "to show that our differences unite us."

With a blistering kick in the last 150 meters, Nikki broke the tape for their 7th national title in 2025 to qualify for the World Championships.

CHAPTER 9

NIKKI HILTZ, TRACK

"CHAMPIONS ADJUST"

GROWING UP IN THE BEACH TOWN OF SANTA CRUZ, California, Nikki Hiltz was the freckled five-foot-four popular kid who always looked out for the underdog in high school. Everybody loved Nikki—senior class president, homecoming queen, and a California state track champion.

As a teenager, it was easy to be what people wanted to see. But Nikki knew that something felt different inside.

It was only on the track where Nikki felt most comfortable. When the bell rang signaling the last lap of a four-lap race, Nikki would shift into an extra gear and sprint past everybody to cross the finish line first. A breathtaking sight to behold.

That final surge is known as the kick, and, today, Nikki's kick is faster and bolder than ever. That's because what's inside now mirrors what's on the outside.

Born female in 1994, Nikki came out publicly at age 26 as transgender nonbinary, using they/them pronouns. It's no coincidence that since Nikki became comfortable with their gender identity, they reached the final of the 2024 Olympic 1,500 meters, won six straight national championships, and are gunning for a medal at the 2028 Los Angeles Olympics.

Confidence and success have made Nikki a leader for the transgender community.

"If you have a purpose or a message, it helps you want it more," Nikki said about winning. "This sport is so mental. I think that my advocacy is my superpower. It's the little thing that gives me the extra boost at the end."

Nikki competes in the women's category in professional track and field because they are biologically female and because there is no nonbinary division. Gradually, the track announcers are getting Nikki's pronouns correct. More than ever, fans are cheering wildly for Nikki during introductions, giving Nikki rainbow hats (for Pride Month), flags, and friendship bracelets—and holding homemade signs like "Here for Hiltz," and "You Belong Everywhere You Decide to Be."

Nikki noticed those particular signs walking onto Franklin Field in Philadelphia for the Grand Slam Track professional meet in May 2025. Minutes before racing, they flashed a huge smile and thumbs-up to the twin sisters who traveled 300 miles to watch their favorite runner compete.

"I don't think I'm ever going to be the best 1,500 runner to ever exist on the women's side," Nikki said after finishing third in the race while nursing a hamstring injury. "But I know that I have a purpose outside of that. It's bigger than just, 'Can I win and break records?' There's a purpose for me being here and doing my best. It's just showing people like, 'Hey, you can be queer and trans and in any space you want.'"

It has taken Nikki 26 years or so to get to a space where they finally feel comfortable on and off the track. The

1,500-meter race is their specialty, a grueling mix of distance running and sprinting that is 100 meters shy of four laps around a track. Nikki's race works perfectly as a metaphor for their career and for their life.

First lap = childhood

Second lap = collegiate career

Third lap = the first four difficult years as a pro

Fourth lap = now

FIRST LAP

NIKKI'S RUNNING CAREER HAS ITS ROOTS ON THE beaches and parks of California's outdoor sports community.

Nikki's father, Tom, was an accomplished marathoner who grew up in Sausalito, outside San Francisco, the son of hippies protesting the Vietnam War in the1960s. Nikki's mother, Liz, grew up playing field hockey on Long Island but was denied a spot on the track team because it was for boys only.

So, when it came time for my Battle of the Sexes match against Bobby Riggs in 1973, Liz Hiltz was part of an eager audience ready to prove that women could compete with men. She and her four sisters loudly cheered over their only brother when I won that match.

Though not a runner, Liz ended up going to the epicenter for college running—the University of Oregon in Eugene. In 1978, Oregon's most famous long-distance runner, Steve Prefontaine, still held cult status three years after his death in a car accident at age 24. Students would flock to watch races at the famed Hayward Field—a place Nikki would get to know well.

Liz and Tom became teachers in California, moving to the coastal city of Santa Cruz.

Michaela was born 18 months before Nikki. The siblings were and are still very close. Nikki wanted to do everything Michaela did.

Michaela joined a popular local program at age six called junior guards, a summer camp that taught lifesaving skills. But when it was their time, Nikki hesitated to join. They liked dressing as a boy and didn't want to wear a girls' bathing suit as a camp uniform. When blowing out the candles on their sixth birthday, they even wished to wake up a boy.

"I feel like my younger self had it all figured out, like they were the Nikki I am now," they said.

It wasn't until the next year that Nikki got the courage to ask their mom to wear a surfing outfit—board shorts and ocean shirt—that was more gender neutral. Liz said yes immediately.

"They didn't see anybody dressed like they wanted to dress," Liz said. "Which just really shows how important it is for athletes to see people playing that look like them,"

In junior guards on Capitola Beach, campers competed in water and beach drills. They performed push-ups and shuttle sprints and competed in ocean swims and paddle board races. Kids would even play dodgeball and capture the flag. Nikki would fly across the beach in running races, leaving the other boys and girls behind in clouds of sand.

"Pure bliss," Nikki said, describing the camp: "A child's dream."

Michaela and Nikki were in different age groups, but Michaela would look across the beach and see Nikki laughing and dominating.

"Nikki is the first person, and everyone else is just behind," Michaela said. "Seeing that, it was like, 'Oh, OK. You're fast. . . . This is something.'"

None of the other kids commented on Nikki's swimwear.

"We both would have been very aware and just shut it down. We were very protective of each other," Michaela said.

People did refer to Nikki as a "tomboy," a term that can be an insult or a compliment—depending on who says it or how. Nikki heard it the way they wanted.

"I have a funny association with that," Nikki said. "I was obviously a tomboy, but my dad's name is Tom. I thought people were saying I'm Tom's boy. Which was kind of gender-affirming for me."

Tom loved that Nikki was a tomboy and had a favorite nickname for his youngest child: "Nickster." Since Nikki was a toddler, they'd be on the back of Tom's bicycle during long rides. In the late 1990s, he stopped competing in marathons and switched to cycling competitions.

Nikki was introduced to the sport of cyclo-cross racing by their dad, Tom, who also competed in the sport.

Tom got Nikki involved in a hybrid sport known as cyclo-cross, in which athletes ride through mud and hills and then jump off to navigate stairs or other obstacles. Tom participated in his age group. As a seven-year-old, Nikki won three races, but it was just a chance to spend more time hanging out with their dad doing a cool hybrid sport.

Nikki preferred to run on the track at the nearby elementary school, announcing in second grade that they wanted to go to the University of Oregon. Liz Hiltz had introduced her children to the greatness (and tragedy) of Prefontaine by repeatedly playing the two films about him. Watching *Without Limits* would later become part of Nikki's pre-race routine.

Soon, Nikki hung two Prefontaine posters on their bedroom wall. Over the years, they also tacked up the bibs they had pinned to their chest during races. Nikki's room was a genuine track-and-field shrine.

While Nikki became a good runner in middle school, it wasn't until they became a freshman at Aptos High School that they thrived. Their running coach, Dan Gruber, a lifelong educator, had led high schoolers like Brett Gotcher to pro careers and was preparing Nikki the same way.

At an early high school meet, Tom Hiltz asked Gruber one simple question: "How good is Nikki?"

Gruber didn't hesitate: "A once-in-a-lifetime talent." All Nikki needed to do, Gruber added, was get into position to out-kick the competition.

Tom remembers one impressive race. Or at least he remembers the tales of it. He didn't see it live because he arrived late from his job as an assistant principal at a nearby high school.

"I missed it by a minute or two so. When I walked on to the scene, you could see lots of people whose jaws were still dropped," Tom said. "They were stunned at the move that Nikki had made with about 200 meters to go to pass the favorite, a senior."

Nikki just smoked by the favorite. "There must have been 10 people telling me their version of what they saw happen. And that was as a freshman. After that, people started going to the meets to watch Nikki race."

Still, as a freshman Nikki didn't find immediate success on the state level, losing in the first round of heats at the California state meet. When Nikki asked Coach Gruber how to improve, he said to get stronger. That summer, the whole track team decided to take Pilates classes. Sort of.

"We were one of those tight-knit teams, so if one person was doing something, we were all going to do it,'" Nikki said. "I just remember laughing the whole time because we'd be on these crazy machines. And all of us were very good athletes, and none of us could do a single one of the activities. To this day, I don't think I could handle a Pilates class."

The Pilates experiment lasted three classes. The laughter still echoes for Nikki, reminding them of the joy they had with their high school teammates.

To stay in shape between the fall cross country and the spring track season, Nikki also played soccer during the winter (both as a midfielder and goalie). And the summers were for Junior Guards.

By junior year, Nikki was setting school records and ranking consistently in the top five among California girls for the 1,600-meter race (the high school distance is four full laps around the 400-meter track).

Their favorite day of the week was Tuesdays when Gruber would do specific drills to improve his team's finishing sprints.

"This sport is so mental. I think that my advocacy is my superpower. It's the little thing that gives me the extra boost at the end."

The Aptos High varsity football players cheered on Nikki to an easy victory during a cross-country meet their junior year.

"On those 150s, you were only practicing gear-shifting," Nikki said. "That's an elite level coaching thing to develop."

The state championships in 2011 were held in Fresno on a weekend when 90-degree temperatures radiated off the rubber composite track. "It felt like you're inside of an oven," Nikki recalled.

Even in the heat, the speed work paid off. Nikki charged to the lead group on the first lap and sat comfortably in fourth place through the second and third laps. When the bell rang for the final lap, nobody could catch Nikki. In those final 150 meters, Nikki sprinted far ahead, finishing in a personal best 4:42.45 seconds. That was more than five seconds ahead of anyone else.

The dream, however, was immediately followed by a nightmare. Nikki's back started aching that night and even more the next day. On the drive home, they developed a high fever, and Liz took her child straight to the emergency room in Santa Cruz. Doctors diagnosed a severe kidney infection.

Hooked up to an IV to rehydrate, Nikki rapidly lost strength. Five days later, they were still on antibiotics but determined to follow through on their plans to fly to New York City to run in a special invitational race: the Adidas Grand Prix Dream Mile organized by Jim Ryun. Ryun was the first United States high school athlete to break the four-minute mile. He also won a silver medal in the 1,500 meters at the 1968 Mexico Olympics.

Gruber cautioned Nikki. "You're not going to be at your best."

Nikki replied with a smile: "It's still an adventure, and it's something I'm not going to get to do again."

On the athletes' bus to the track, Nikki made sure to sit next to Ethiopia's Tirunesh Dibaba, who had become the first woman to win gold medals in the 5,000 meters and 10,000 meters at the 2008 Beijing Olympics. Nikki picked her brain on becoming an Olympian.

When it came time for the high school race, Nikki finished last, in fourteenth place.

Nikki recovered, but, weeks later while on the beach working as a Junior Guard counselor, they felt a lingering foot pain. Doctors confirmed a stress fracture, meaning no running for six months.

Nikki redirected their energies to serving as president of their 400-person senior class and was even elected to the homecoming court. When Nikki and their boyfriend at the time, Joey, were named king and queen of the court, they were quite the pair. Joey was on crutches, having just injured his leg in the first half of the football game. He threw on a white jacket over his uniform. Nikki, wearing a white dress, was also on crutches recovering from foot surgery.

As per Aptos High tradition, the freshmen players carried the king and queen off the field. "Don't drop these people—they're already injured!" the public address announcer shouted.

Today, Nikki laughs at their high school memory of wearing a dress and sporting wavy, mid-length strawberry blond hair.

"That was the most straight, cisgender thing ever—not me at all," Nikki said. (Cisgender describes a person who identifies with the gender they were assigned at birth.)

"I feel like in order to survive, I needed to go into these boxes," Nikki said. "So, in junior high and high school I felt, to be safe and maybe not get bullied or be othered, I'm going to present feminine and have boyfriends even if I'm not attracted to men. I made those decisions based on wanting to feel like I belonged when, in reality, true belonging is just being yourself."

Outwardly, Nikki seemed to be having a great time in high school. They loved being silly and social, refusing to sacrifice typical high school activities for track meets.

Nikki was on the organizing committee for the prom which featured an "Under the Sea" theme. (The tables featured live goldfish in fishbowls.) Nikki designed a clever proposal to ask a boyfriend from another school to the prom: by dressing up in a cow costume. When he came out of school, Nikki held up a sign: "Got Prom?" copying the "Got Milk?" ad.

Never mind that Nikki had a regional qualifying meet the morning after prom. They loved dancing with their friends, and, the next day, they won the regional meet.

By then, Nikki was already returning to running form despite missing more than six months of training. At the state championship, Nikki finished as runner-up, one-half second behind the winner.

SECOND LAP

NIKKI ACCEPTED A SCHOLARSHIP TO RUN AT THE University of Oregon, their dream. But when competing for Oregon's Cross Country team that fall, Nikki injured their other foot and needed surgery. It was a lonely time as Nikki rehabbed during a cold, rainy winter. While Nikki eventually returned to competing, they were disappointed when Oregon reduced its scholarship money. Nikki transferred to the track powerhouse, the University of Arkansas, where they were given a full scholarship.

As a junior, Nikki won the competitive Southeastern Conference title at 1,500 meters. At the NCAA championships, they finished second, earning all-American honors. They would finish their college career as a seven-time all-American, including honors in both indoor and outdoor track and field.

Success came at a time when Nikki was feeling more secure in their personal life. Nikki started dating a woman on the Arkansas team, and they both were captains. Nikki was relieved when the two came out to their unsurprised teammates, and then each came out as gay to their parents on the same day in 2016.

Nikki, Tom, and Liz were on the deck of a restaurant in Lake Tahoe. They were not surprised either. "Great," Tom said. "What are we going to eat?"

In retrospect, Liz felt sad that Nikki didn't feel comfortable saying anything sooner. "We raised Nikki in Santa Cruz County, one of the most liberal counties probably in the country," Liz Hiltz said. "The only church we ever took them to, the pastor was a Black, gay woman. They knew they were in a safe environment. I hope they didn't think they were disappointing us, because they certainly weren't."

With strong parental support and a strong relationship, Nikki excelled on the track and was invited to run in the 2017 US Track and Field Championships in Sacramento. It was not a collegiate race, so Nikki didn't have a coach there.

Liz became her daughter's unofficial stats person and team psychologist, looking up Nikki's competitors to check season-best times. Liz did the math and figured Nikki's finishing times would beat many of them. In the hotel before the race, she texted Nikki her scouting report, and added a motivational quote for good measure:

"Racing teaches us to challenge ourselves. It teaches us to push beyond where we thought we could go. It helps us to find out what we are made of. This is what we do. This is what it's all about." —PattiSue Plumer (two-time US Olympian)

Nikki finished sixth with a personal best time of 4:10.28, the top time for any collegiate runner. Liz decided she would keep texting Nikki before every race. The tradition continues today, with Liz often recycling quotes that led to winning races and discarding ones that didn't.

Being a professional runner is not like having a desk job. Athletes earn money for winning races, as well as for just entering races—and those races are spread out throughout the year. Runners earn most of their money by signing with shoe and apparel companies.

After graduating from Arkansas with a degree in sociology and criminal justice, Nikki signed a three-year endorsement deal with Adidas in 2018 that afforded a living and training setup in San Diego. Nikki made an impressive pro debut, winning the 2019 US Road Mile Championship and qualifying for the finals of the 1,500 meters at the world championships. The 2020 Tokyo Olympics beckoned.

Except, of course, the COVID pandemic hit in 2020, and life changed dramatically. Running was still possible, but with no social interaction, Nikki was struggling. The relationship with their college girlfriend came to an end.

As many people were doing at the time, Nikki found comfort in online communities and scrolled through TikTok. One day, Nikki saw a playful post from Emma Gee, the first publicly out LGBTQ+ athlete at Brigham Young University (BYU). Nikki slid into her DMs.

Emma, who had grown up Mormon, was in Provo, Utah (the home of BYU). The two struck up a long-distance friendship that turned into a romantic relationship. Emma moved to San Diego.

By then, Nikki was already deep into planning a virtual race—where participants competed on their own 5-kilometer course—that would also be a fundraiser for queer youth in

Nikki and their partner, professional runner Emma Gee, posed in the shirts for the Pride 5K run. Nikki started the race in 2020 to raise money for support for LGBTQ+ youth. "We belong everywhere we decide to be," read the 2024 T-shirts.

need. Nikki and friends, including Emma, organized a Pride 5K for people to run around the world on the same day in 2020.

Nikki designed the first T-shirt ("Love More Than Ever," it read in rainbow colors) and sent it to participants who ran the 5K on their own. Nearly 2,000 runners completed the race, raising $33,000 for The Trevor Project, an organization that provides crisis counseling and suicide intervention for LGBTQ+ youth.

The Pride 5K continues as an annual event, both virtually and in-person.

The race gave Nikki purpose just as they were figuring out who they were. One day during the height of the pandemic, Nikki was scrolling TikTok when a video popped up in their "For You" page titled, "What does it mean to be nonbinary?"

Wow. This made sense. "I finally had the language for what I had been feeling my entire life," Nikki said.

On March 31, 2021, the International Transgender Day of Visibility, Nikki made it public, posting this on Instagram:

"Hi I'm Nikki and I'm transgender. That means I don't identify with the gender I was assigned at birth. The word I use currently to describe my gender is nonbinary. The best way I can explain my gender is as fluid. Sometimes I wake up feeling like a powerful queen and other days I wake up feeling as if I'm just a guy being a dude, and other times I identify outside of the gender binary entirely. It's complicated and complex and something I'm still trying to navigate myself, but I've decided it's time to share my gender fluidity with you all. Posting this is both exciting and terrifying but I am and always will be a firm believer that vulnerability and visibility are essential in creating social change and acceptance. So here I am, once again, coming out of a closet to be my true authentic self."

When Nikki came out for a second time—as transgender nonbinary—their parents were again supportive.

"Nikki certainly didn't do a big turnaround on us, where they were dressing in princess clothes, and makeup. They've always presented this way, so, it's just Nikki," Liz said. "They are who they are, and you just love them."

Liz encouraged Nikki with powerful words: "Those who mind won't matter and those who matter won't mind."

THIRD LAP

TOM AND LIZ WERE—AND STILL ARE—VERY concerned about the online hate that Nikki received on social media. Nikki has learned to block the worst trolls but still saw the bigoted and spiteful comments from strangers. Nikki was also worried about how the track community would react. And the Tokyo Olympic Trials were looming.

"For those three months, I was really paranoid of how I was going to be perceived and received by others in the community, in the track and field world," Nikki said. "Am I going to be a burden? Is it going to be annoying for the NBC announcers to have to remember to use 'they/them' pronouns? Will the meet director be annoyed that I'm there because now they have to use inclusive language?"

Nikki was back at Hayward Field at the University of Oregon for the 2021 Olympic Trials. They were struggling emotionally but were worse off physically. Nikki was up the night before their race with a hacking cough. They advanced through the heats only to finish last in the final. They didn't go to Tokyo.

The crushing disappointment lingered, and there were

looming contract decisions. By the end of 2021, Nikki decided not to re-sign with Adidas when the contract expired.

"I wanted to work with a brand that cared about me and my athletic performances, but also what I'm doing off of the track," Nikki said.

Instead, Nikki was one of the first professional runners to sign with Lululemon. More changes were coming. At the end of 2021, Nikki and Emma moved from San Diego to Flagstaff, Arizona, to be coached by Mike Smith, who was also the coach of Northern Arizona University's track team. Emma was pursuing her running career, too.

Everything was an adjustment, starting with the altitude—6,821 feet above sea level. The altitude made Nikki's lungs work harder but over the months made them stronger.

Nikki entered the 2023 US Track and Field Championships back in Oregon in peak condition. On the starting line for the 1,500 meters, Nikki spotted a fan in the Hayward Field stands holding the pink, blue, and white transgender pride flag.

"That person is at a sporting event brave enough to hold a trans flag, that's a huge deal," Nikki said. "Maybe they got the courage to do that because of me. And that means I already won the race. I feel like it freed me up so much because my 'why' has already been accomplished."

After winning the championship, Nikki went to the fan holding the flag and gave that person the bib. It said "Hiltz," and so much more.

"I don't think Nikki set out to be a role model," high school coach Dan Gruber said. "I think Nikki just finally got to the point of, 'I need to be myself.' And by being that strong, taking the hits for people, maybe the people that follow Nikki will not have to take the hits as bad."

FOURTH LAP

WHEN THE BELL RINGS FOR THE FINAL LAP OF A race, it's Nikki's favorite sound in the world.

"I remember this feeling setting my soul on fire when I raced my first ever mile on the track when I was 13 years old," Nikki posted on Instagram.

In 2023, it's like a bell went off inside Nikki's mind. Their career took off.

Nikki stormed to an American mile record, running 4:16.35 at an international meet in Monaco. A month later at the 2023 World Track and Field Championships in Budapest, Nikki was standing on the starting line for the first heat when they saw a familiar face in the stands. Their high school coach, Dan Gruber, had surprised his star athlete. Nikki flashed the heart sign to him. They did not make the final.

Still, Nikki felt like they were moving into prime position to make the 2024 US Olympic Team. Their coach, Mike Smith, was careful to remove the pressure before the trials. Neither was allowed to utter the "O word" (Olympics).

The Olympic trials would be on the familiar Hayward Field. Nikki's 1,500-meter final would be on the last day of June, celebrated as Pride Month.

At the time, Nikki's partner Emma was training to make the Olympic team in the steeplechase (a middle-distance race with hurdles and a water obstacle). When she did not qualify, Emma switched into support mode for Nikki. She could sense a difference in her partner.

"They had really owned their situation for three years going into the Olympic trials," Emma said. "They'd been working on those skillsets and had me and their family."

Emma added: "They had built enough stability in their support system and in their training that they could go in and compete to the best of their ability."

In the final lap of the race to qualify for the Olympics, Nikki waited to make a move until the last 100 meters. Nikki navigated to an outside lane and—as only they can do—passed several runners and finally rocketed past rival Elle Purrier St. Pierre for the victory. Nikki set a US Olympic Trials record, running a personal best 3:55.33.

"This is bigger than just me," Nikki said, beaming during an interview with NBC. "Last day of Pride Month . . . All the LGBTQ folks brought me home that last 100."

At the Paris Olympics in 2024, Nikki advanced to the finals of the 1,500 meters, a race dominated by non-Americans for a decade. In the final race, under the lights, Nikki followed their game plan perfectly. But when it came time to kick, everyone else in the field was just too fast. Nikki hung on for seventh place out of 12 runners—and finished as the top American with a time of 3:56:38. Kenya's Faith Kipyegon won gold by running more than five seconds faster—in 3:51.29. Nikki knows they will always be chasing Faith.

When fans said, "Sorry you didn't get a medal," Nikki shrugged it off.

"That's your level measure of success, that's not mine," Nikki said. "I've never gone out that hard before in a race. I'm so proud that I just committed to the fast pace and wasn't afraid."

In the winter of 2025, Nikki built on their Olympic success at home by winning two indoor US championships—the 1,500 meters and the 3,000 meters. Nikki re-signed with Lululemon and then hired a new coach, one who was already coaching Emma: Juli Benson. Coach Benson, herself a track Olympian in 1996, went on to coach Jenny Simpson. In 2011, Simpson won a women's world championship at 1,500 meters—the last US runner to do so.

With Benson's guidance, Nikki stormed to a 2025 outdoor national championship in the 1,500 meters at Hayward Field. Once again, Nikki found another gear with 150 meters to go, slipping through traffic and bursting to the lead in the backstretch, finishing in 4:03.15.

Nikki would only get faster from there. In August 2025, Nikki won their first race on the top international circuit known as the Diamond League. In Brussels, they ran a blistering 3:55.94, surging past Australian Linden Hall. It was their fastest time of the season.

In September 2025, Nikki made the 1,500-meter final of the world track-and-field championships in Tokyo. Faith Kipyegon ran away with gold, finishing in 3:52.15, and Nikki finished in fifth place in 3:57.33. Nikki was disappointed not to get a medal but also recognized that fifth in the world championships was their highest placing. Unlike one-day track meets, the Olympics and world championships both require runners to advance through two qualifying rounds and that takes strategy to keep their legs fresh.

"You can't skip steps in this sport, you have to do little increments," Nikki told the media in Tokyo, referring to their eleventh-place finish at the 2023 World Championships, and their seventh-place finish at the 2024 Paris Olympics.

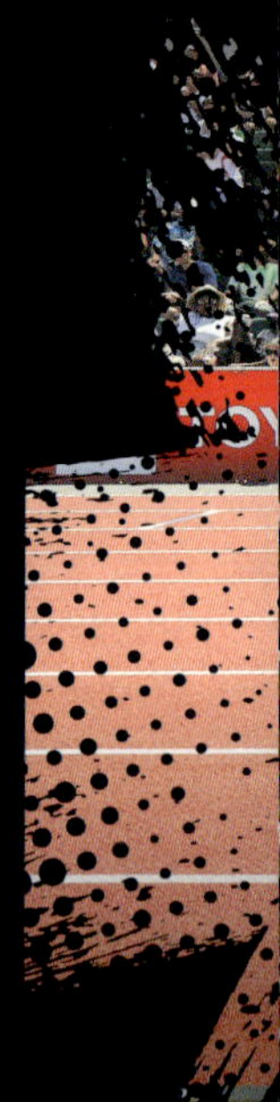

Nikki (No. 12) tucked into a pack during the 1,500 meters of the 2025 US national championships. It was only a matter of time until Nikki made their signature move in the final lap.

They are very familiar with incremental change and not always for the better. The climate in professional running has become increasingly political around the issue of gender. Track and field's international governing body, World Athletics, has prohibited athletes who were born male and transitioned to female—transgender women—from competing, saying that it would be an unfair advantage. The president of World Athletics even wants to institute sex tests for all female athletes.

That won't be an issue for Nikki because they have no desire now to take male hormones—like testosterone—because that would be illegal in competition. Nikki revealed on social media that they did have top surgery (in September 2024) to make their breasts flatter to align better with their gender identity.

In 2025, President Trump signed an executive order banning trans women from competing in school sports. The NCAA followed, even though it acknowledged that out of 500,000 college athletes, only 10 were trans women. The Republican-led Congress at the time was debating bills—and, in some states, passing them—banning gender-affirming health care for trans youth.

"To all the trans people reading this post right now I want you to know that even though they are banning a lot of things in order to make our lives far more difficult than necessary, one thing they can never ban is our trans joy," Nikki wrote on social media.

Nikki often posts uplifting educational videos breaking down terms like "transgender" and "nonbinary"—not just for their 260K+ followers, but more for the parents of their audience. Nikki explained why.

"Our country right now is so divided, . . . and I don't want to lose the people in the middle," Nikki said. "I really think that there's value in saying, 'Hey, where can we find this meeting place?' And I think a lot of it comes back to a lack of education and maybe someone's just never had the opportunity to even know what the word 'nonbinary' means."

Nikki said that while this lesson may not work for people unwilling to listen, a "ton of people" reached out saying they sent this post to their parents, and it really helped them understand.

"I feel like sports have the ability or power to set the stage for what's possible," Nikki said. "Of course, I want to inspire younger athletes and queer athletes to be themselves and chase their big, scary dreams. But I also want to empower someone who's maybe not an athlete and just watching the Olympics, to say, 'Wow, this person is showing up in their place of work, and their pronouns are getting respected.' We can get it right, and it's such a simple thing. You can make other people feel loved and accepted."

Nikki is feeling the love and support more than ever because people are joining them in the fight. "In a weird way, even though it's probably the darkest time for trans Americans," they said, "I have never felt more sure of myself, that I belong here."

Chelsea lifted her Duke Blue Devils to three conference championships and was named an All-America selection for her sophomore and junior years before a fractured kneecap ended her college career.

CHAPTER 10

CHELSEA GRAY, BASKETBALL

"STARTS WITH INTEGRITY"

JAMES AND VICKEY GRAY HUNG A SIGN ON THE inside of their daughter Chelsea's childhood bedroom door: "Starts with Family."

She hardly needed a reminder. The outward signs of the Gray family motto were all around her.

Chelsea was always playing basketball with her brother and cousins on neighborhood courts in the Oakland area of California. Her mom and dad alternated shifts at their night jobs so they could watch Chelsea play in high school. Her aunt hosted sleepovers in Hayward so Chelsea could stay late at the courts with her cousins. Her grandmother took teenage Chelsea to the airport on weekends to play for her club team in Los Angeles.

Decades later, in June 2025 when Chelsea returned to the San Francisco Bay Area as a decorated point guard for the WNBA's Las Vegas Aces, about 50 of her family members and friends packed a fancy suite at the Chase Center to support her.

Everyone was wearing Chelsea Gray gear from the different stops of her 11-year pro career: a No. 12 red Aces jersey; a No. 8 red USA Olympic jersey; a T-shirt celebrating her gold medal from the 2024 Paris Olympics; a black-and-white leather jacket from the Aces' 2022 championship season, when Chelsea was named MVP of the WNBA Finals; and her green No. 12 jersey from Unrivaled, the women's 3-on-3 winter league in Miami, where Chelsea was also named MVP of those finals.

"She's the best thing, the one that really keeps our family together," said Chelsea's older brother, Javon. "Whenever my parents have a bad day, they watch one of Chelsea's games. Even if they watched this same game 10 times, they feel the energy. She makes everything better."

Former teammate Candace Parker nicknamed Chelsea "The Point Gawd" for her OMG-worthy passes and because she sees all on the court.

"I think it's the nature of my position and how I look at sports and life," Chelsea said. "How can I make the next person better? By making others better and by challenging them, I've made my own greatness."

Chelsea Gray knows she is not the most famous name on her Las Vegas team—that honor goes to four-time league MVP forward A'ja Wilson. But in getting Wilson the ball and in creating opportunities for all of her Aces teammates, Chelsea led Las Vegas to a 2025 championship, their third in four years. That made Chelsea the only active WNBA player with four titles (she won one with Los Angeles in 2016). Chelsea also has two Olympic gold medals and has been named to six All-Star teams.

She's easy to recognize. Chelsea's the one who runs up court with her knees pointed inward, her feet scuffing the floor like she's wearing flip-flops instead of her Player Exclusive shoes. She's also rocketing no-look passes, picking the pocket of opposing point guards, and flexing with a full-throated yell after every great play.

Coaches, general managers, and the 179 other players across the league know No. 12 as the smartest basketball player on the court. Chelsea is a throwback to when point guards were true floor leaders, passing first and shooting 3-pointers with the game on the line.

"Whether it's NBA, WNBA, there's very few players with vision like hers, she just has a gift," said Las Vegas Aces coach Becky Hammon, a Hall of Fame former point guard. "Her mind and her competitiveness set her apart. That's really her greatness."

In another important way, Chelsea represents the past, present, and future of women's pro basketball.

She and her wife, Tipesa, are married and are parents to a young son. As a LGBTQ+ Black athlete, Chelsea is part of the generation of basketball players who are normalizing being gay in a league that did not always support lesbian culture. Today, she has endorsement deals because of—not despite—her sexual orientation.

She and Tipesa starred in a commercial for Whirlpool washers and dryers because young parents do a lot of laundry. You can't get more normal than that.

"I think my living out my truth is part of the resistance and part of changing people's lives," Chelsea said. "I would hope that later down the line, there's not a part of you that has to come out, because it's kind of normal. It's just who you are and your journey and your story and what your family looks like."

Chelsea at three years old. Her mom, Vickey Gray, would take her to get formal photographs every six months.

JAVON GRAY WAS 10 YEARS OLD WHEN HIS SISTER Chelsea was born in 1992. He became her first coach and biggest fan.

By the time Chelsea was tall enough to bounce a basketball (age four), she was watching Javon and their older cousin, Steven Crawford, play in driveways and local parks, waiting her turn. Soon, another cousin, Sean Watkins (four years younger than Chelsea), tagged along. The four were always a unit and even today consider themselves siblings.

Chelsea's mom, Vickey, worked the overnight shift as a corrections officer in San Jose, an hour from their home in Manteca, a town in California's Central Valley. Chelsea's dad, James, often worked late as a printer at a graphic design company.

On Fridays, Chelsea would hop in Javon's car to go an hour west to Oakland where her aunt and grandparents lived. There, Chelsea would play basketball with the boys on the playground until the sun set. Sometimes on weekends, she and her cousin Sean would go fishing with their grandfather, competing to see who could catch the most catfish.

When Javon organized neighborhood games on Mondays back in Manteca, he and Chelsea would prepare tacos and put sodas on ice, selling them while the games were going on. (Today Chelsea loves to make tacos for her family.)

When it was their turn to take the court, Javon always picked Chelsea. The other boys would laugh. Sean would shake his head and tell those boys:

"You chose the wrong decision, man. You should have picked her up first, because now we're about to run this whole park."

Never mind that, at nine years old, she was the only girl on the court—a foot shorter and at least five years younger than most guys. Chelsea was their secret weapon because no one could pass like she could. Going backdoor, behind-the-back passes, or lobbing it down the court, Chelsea delivered passes no one else saw coming.

That was by necessity. In playground rules, said Sean: "You had to be good enough or you were not going to play."

Chelsea loved proving herself. "I wasn't afraid of a challenge," she said. "And I think that really stuck with me, because at a young age, I was around these big guys, and I was playing with them. They gave me that confidence that I could hoop with anybody."

When they moved and could no longer use the driveway hoops of their neighbors, James installed a basket at their new house. Chelsea practiced so much that the fiberglass backboard started to crack. So, Chelsea used the pole instead to practice her passing. With her back to the basket, she had to whip the ball in just the right spot so it would ricochet back to her. Otherwise, it would clank into the street, and she'd have to run after it.

When she mastered that drill, she upped the degree of difficulty. Chelsea substituted the basketball for a tennis ball to practice her accuracy and her artistry.

"It just was me free-flowing and playing in the yard. The creativity of it was fun for me," she said.

Chelsea first played on a boys' team at the local boys and girls club at age eight. When she was 10, she signed up for the only girls' club team in the area, even though it was for teenagers. Even then, she had "handles"—dribbling skills so smooth she rarely turned the ball over.

Chelsea would spend hours studying pro players,

following her multiple role models, including point guard Ticha Penicheiro. Penicheiro played an hour up the road for the Sacramento Monarchs, one of the eight original WNBA teams.

Above her bed, she had a poster of Cynthia Cooper, the MVP guard who led the Houston Comets to the first four WNBA championships. Chelsea read her autobiography cover to cover.

Chelsea also loved to study videos of Hall of Famer Magic Johnson, the former guard for the Los Angeles Lakers. Chelsea's dazzling passing earned her the nickname "Lady Magic" when she got to high school.

"I just kind of fell in love with the art of passing, in watching Ticha play, watching Magic Johnson play," Chelsea said. "I love the illusion, and how you can fake a whole arena out and only you and that other person kind of figure out where the ball is going."

There was a fourth player she adored, an NBA icon in the early 2000s: Allen Iverson of the Philadelphia 76ers, who was the league's 2001 MVP.

Javon bought Iverson's signature "Answer" shoes by Reebok. Back then, the shoes came with a DVD of Iverson breaking down his famous crossover dribble—he'd bounce the ball between his legs, dribble with his left, then his right, spin or step back and hit a jumper. It was the kind of move that would catch defenders flat-footed or cause them to fall down.

Chelsea, Javon, and Sean all perfected the crossover by bouncing the ball on the living room carpet while watching the DVD.

"I liked that you thought he was going one way and then going the other," Chelsea said. "I just made it my own."

She also copied Iverson's style as a basketball player and as someone who wore his hair in tight braids and recorded rap music. “The way he carried himself, he was unapologetically himself,” Chelsea said. “His braiding style was super dope to me. My brother had corn rows, I had corn rows.”

She and Sean both wore Iverson’s No. 3 from middle school through high school. When Chelsea got to college, the No. 3 jersey was taken. She and her dad discussed it. Since 1+2=3, she would be No. 12.

At the 2025 NBA All-Star Game in San Francisco, Chelsea finally got to meet her hero. Actually, Iverson approached her. “Chelsea Gray! You are my favorite player,” he said. Chelsea was so humbled by meeting her idol, she just smiled and said thank you, posing for some pictures that her family and friends keep on their phones.

Game recognizes game.

- - - - ★ - - - -

ST. MARY’S HIGH SCHOOL IN STOCKTON, CALIFORNIA had long been a powerhouse before Chelsea arrived at the parochial school located 20 minutes from her home. The program’s greatness coincided with Chelsea’s own growth spurt. Between her sophomore and junior years, she grew to five-foot-eleven from five-foot-seven, making her much harder to defend.

In her final two seasons, she led the Rams to two state championships and was named a McDonald’s All-American. As a senior, Chelsea was the Parade Magazine Co-National Player of the Year (sharing honors with future WNBA All-Star center and ESPN broadcaster, Chiney Ogwumike from Texas). St. Mary’s was ranked No. 1 in the country during Chelsea’s senior season, and she finished her career with 2,164 points and averaged 6.1 assists per game.

"I really love making other people shine and making them better. A lot of people can score the basketball. There's only so many that can pass the way I pass."

Chelsea led Saint Mary's High School in Stockton, California, to state championships in 2009 and 2010. Her No. 3 jersey was retired in 2022.

"It was never about her; it was about the team," Alle Moreno, her teammate and the current St. Mary's coach, told KCRA-TV in 2022, when the school retired Chelsea's jersey. "It was never about her stats; it was about winning, and that goes to show who she is as a person."

Even when Chelsea hit a memorable game-winning shot to clinch the Northern California high school championship, she did not want that moment to be her legacy.

"It's not that I don't enjoy making last second shots, the thrill of it all is just amazing," she said. "I really love making other people shine and making them better. A lot of people can score the basketball. There's only so many that can pass the way I pass."

Chelsea refined her game playing in the spring and summer with the top club team in the state which competed in the Nike Elite Youth Basketball League. When the coach, George Quintero, first traveled from Los Angeles on a recruiting visit to St. Mary's, he saw Chelsea exceling in drills. He also saw those knock-knees. He joked with Vickey Gray that he was going to change her daughter's running form and immediately gave Chelsea an invite to join his team.

On weekends in the spring and summer, Chelsea would fly to Los Angeles to play with the team and lived with the Quintero family in Santa Clarita. Vickey and James felt comfortable having their daughter stay with them. Soon, they became Chelsea's second family. She still calls Quintero, "Pops."

"Chelsea was loyal to being special," Quintero said. "She wanted to be the best passer in women's basketball."

Chelsea might have seemed serious in her devotion to her craft, but once she warmed up to teammates, she was a jokester who would keep her coaches and players loose.

She is still the designated DJ in the locker room where she proudly blasts Bay Area artists.

Her playfulness was key to her creativity. Quintero and his son and daughter would take Chelsea bowling, where she had the most unique shot. Chelsea would start her approach, then jump to the lane on the left and launch the ball with such wicked spin that it bounced down the alley, hooked left, and knocked down the pins.

When they went go-karting together, Chelsea took to the course like a Formula One driver. "She handled her business in a way I couldn't catch her," Quintero said, laughing. "She wouldn't let me get behind or in front of her. She just has a gift. And it's the nuance that you can't describe why someone is so crafty, the fact that she could spin a ball off a backboard in the way that she does."

Chelsea's instincts went beyond seeing the action on the court. One year, Quintero hired a successful area coach to be his assistant. Within days, Chelsea whispered to Quintero, "He's not good for us."

She was right. The girls didn't respond to his arrogance. And he was gone.

Another year in Los Angeles, Quintero took Chelsea to play with two boys' teams. "You could see they weren't interested. Like they were wondering, 'Why do we have this chick on the court?'" Quintero recalled.

The opposing team had a center looming impossibly tall at six-foot-six-inches, a teenage boy who had just broken a backboard at Santa Monica High School dunking the ball. Chelsea was not intimidated.

"She goes by him with a wraparound, behind-the-back-move down the lane," Quintero recalled. "Then he tries to block her shot, and Chelsea does her classic teardrop in the air, floats the ball over him, and scores. The whole place went nuts, and all the boys went nuts. And that's how she established, number one, I could play here, and number two, I'm just as good as all of you."

AT ST. MARY'S, A COLLEGE PREP SCHOOL, CHELSEA was also a top student and an academic all-American with a 3.7 GPA. She could have gone to the academic and athletic powerhouse nearby, Stanford University. Or the University of California, Berkeley, where her cousin, Alexis Gray-Lawson, had played basketball five years earlier. But Chelsea wanted to challenge herself by leaving the safety net of her family.

"I wanted to do something super different and kind of push the boundaries at a young age," she said.

The Duke University Women's Basketball Program was not as famous as the men's, but, at the time, Coach Joanne P. McCallie was assembling top-level talent. She needed Chelsea to make her 2010 recruiting class No. 1 in the country. McCallie brought in a Duke superstar to close the deal. On Chelsea's recruiting visit to Duke, Mike Krzyzewski, the Hall of Fame men's basketball coach, was waiting for her and her parents in the famous Cameron Indoor Stadium on campus.

"Chelsea Gray!" Krzyzewski shouted from across the court.

When Chelsea's dad shook hands with Coach K (as he's known), the coach smiled at James and nodded to Chelsea: "This here is something special," he said.

Then Coach K pulled Chelsea aside and gave her the pitch: "This is going to be one of the greatest decisions that you ever make in your life, just coming to Duke and putting on that jersey and being part of our family. Once a Blue Devil, always a Blue Devil. And you won't regret wearing that jersey or going to school here."

After Chelsea committed to be a Blue Devil, digital outlet HoopGurlz ranked Duke's 2010 recruiting class as top in the nation.

Chelsea's mom Vickey was anxious about sending her daughter 2,700 miles across the country. But Vickey made friends with a local hotel manager in Durham, North Carolina, so she could visit and watch her daughter play whenever possible. Family first.

In her first two seasons, Chelsea was a standout player and was named to the Atlantic Coast Conference first team as a sophomore. She was off to a tremendous start junior year, but a few weeks before the NCAA Tournament in February 2013, Chelsea dislocated her right kneecap coming down awkwardly from a rebound. She screamed out in severe pain, knowing her promising season was over. Chelsea had been so dominant up to that point that she was still named a co-conference player of the year.

Chelsea returned the next season, but she reinjured the knee. This time, she fractured the kneecap, a more serious setback. Her collegiate playing career was over. But her contributions to the program were not; she became an unofficial assistant coach for Coach McCallie.

Chelsea graduated with a degree in sociology and African American studies, while obtaining a certificate in markets and management studies. Yet she still wanted basketball to be her career and convinced her parents that she was going to succeed.

"My whole thing was education, and she did very well in school," her mom said. "So, what do you do? You let her do what she loves."

The Connecticut Sun selected Chelsea No. 11 in the 2014 draft, even though they knew she would sit out the season to rehab the knee. The team paid her a portion of her rookie salary, but it was not enough to pay her living expenses, so she made alternate plans.

Quintero offered Chelsea a job as an assistant coach running skills camps in Los Angeles and, again, a spot in his home. That time would also give Chelsea the chance to develop a life-changing relationship.

CHELSEA HAD WATCHED A GAME AT LONG BEACH State in 2010 when she first met Tipesa Mercedes Moorer, a six-foot forward who played from 2008 to 2012 and later became the program's director of basketball operations.

"The first thing that I noticed—and is still one of my favorite things to this day—is her smile," Tipesa said. "We started talking, and that's when I was really like, okay, she's interesting, she's attractive, and she's funny. That's really what kind of drew me in."

In 2014, while Chelsea was coaching youth players and doing physical therapy, she and Tipesa began dating. When Chelsea signed with a team in Israel to get professional experience in the offseason before joining the WNBA, Tipesa traveled with her. She would later go with Chelsea to Spain and Turkey.

(Even a decade ago, this was quite common for WNBA players to go overseas to supplement their salaries. An athlete's body can only last a limited number of years, so players want to maximize their career opportunities.)

For the 2016 WNBA season, Chelsea was traded to the Los Angeles Sparks. And that was where Chelsea's career ignited. With Tipesa in the stands, Chelsea came off the bench to help the Sparks win a championship.

Chelsea kept her relationship with Tipesa quiet at first, mulling how to tell her parents that she was dating a woman, but still recognizing how important Tipesa was to her.

"We kind of grew up together," Chelsea said. "As I've grown in this league, as a person and off the court, she's been everywhere, to a lot of appearances, a lot of trips in my life. I'm leaving out a big portion of who I am if I don't mention my relationship and being with her."

Tipesa had already come out to her family and was more confident in her identity. But Chelsea wasn't ready.

"It was not the norm, and I hid it for a while," Chelsea recalled. "I didn't know what life would look like later. It took me a long time to feel comfortable."

Swallowing her nervousness, Chelsea texted her mom first: "Mom, can we talk?"

Then she called her. "Mom, I've done everything right that you and dad have taught me to do and to be," Chelsea began.

Her mom agreed. Chelsea then told her about Tipesa.

Her mother answered, "Yeah, I'm shocked. But Chelsea, are you happy?"

Chelsea said she was. It took mother and daughter some time, a "journey" to getting to where they are today, as Chelsea called it.

Her father, James, expressed a truism of the LGBTQ+ community: "Love is love."

Chelsea and Tipesa, smiling brightly and embracing lovingly in an Instagram post, announced their engagement in 2018. They were married the next year in Bel Air, California. At the wedding, her brother Javon gave a speech admitting that he and his cousins checked out Tipesa like amateur investigators, making sure Tipesa was good enough for their sister. Javon even looked up Tipesa's college basketball stats.

It was clear to Tipesa that Chelsea's brother and cousins meant everything to her. "They always show up when it matters and when it counts," Tipesa said. "And I think that unwavering support was foundational in the confidence that she has in herself and her ability to just go after whatever she wants. They're definitely a huge reason that she is like that."

Tipesa and Chelsea navigated the pandemic together and moved to Bradenton, Florida, where the WNBA played its delayed 2020 season in the security of a bubble (nicknamed the "Wubble").

In 2021, following five years in Los Angeles, Chelsea felt it was time for a change. She signed a contract with the Aces, a franchise that had recently relocated from San Antonio to Las Vegas. Fans and coaches named Chelsea to the WNBA All-Star team her first year in Vegas.

But the next year, coaches and fans selected players with better statistics. Her game changed because of it.

"I thought I had played well enough to be an all-star, but it also was humbling, and I just went to work," Chelsea said. "I got in even better shape. I've focused on all of the little things to be ready for the playoffs and win a championship."

In 2022, the Las Vegas Aces won the first of three championships. Chelsea was named the Finals MVP, and she averaged 18.3 points and 6 assists per game.

The bonus money from winning the MVP and the league title meant Chelsea did not need to go to Europe to earn money in the offseason. Hoping to gain broadcasting experience for her post-playing career, she signed to be an analyst for a college basketball television network in Durham, North Carolina, home to her alma mater Duke.

CHELSEA GRAY

Chelsea helped lead the Las Vegas Aces to three WNBA titles from 2022 to 2025. She has a fourth from her time with the Los Angeles Sparks.

Chelsea proved she could rebound from her collegiate injuries, playing in 283 of 284 games in her first eight seasons in the WNBA—until Game Three of the 2023 Finals against the New York Liberty. In the fourth quarter, she felt her left foot pop; it turned out to be a fracture.

In Game Four of the series, Chelsea had a boot on her foot and wore crutches. She called plays from the bench and was active in the huddle. When her teammates clinched the championship, Chelsea threw her crutches to the sideline and hobbled out to join her teammates in a celebratory pile on the court.

She had foot surgery soon after, which turned out to be tough timing. When Tipesa, gave birth to their son, Lennox, in February of 2024, Chelsea's movement was limited. She was unable to fully help Tipesa in their first months of motherhood.

Chelsea worked feverishly to rehabilitate from surgery and returned to the Aces' lineup in June of 2024. She was named to her second US Olympic squad and was a starting guard for the gold-medal winning Team USA.

In August, Adidas released her player-exclusive shoe that she designed: lavender for Tipesa's favorite color, orange for Chelsea's, and sage green for Lennox's. His nickname is Wolf, so there's a pawprint on the back of the heel, along with "Point Gawd" printed on the side.

The name of the shoe? "Family First."

Unsurprisingly, Chelsea is a natural mother, bringing her point guard personality home. "She's patient, she's calm, she loves teaching him new things," Tipesa said, adding that Chelsea also loves to goof around with Lennox: "She's the same way that she's animated on the court."

Vickey and James now make more trips to Las Vegas—to watch their grandson play as well as their daughter.

"With Lennox, I can see how people gravitate towards him the same way they gravitated towards Chelsea," James said. "He's outgoing, fun, and loveable."

By the winter of 2025, Chelsea was fully healthy and happy. She was thrilled that she didn't have to go overseas or look to broadcasting for an offseason job. Instead, Chelsea got to play in a new women's professional basketball league, Unrivaled, founded by two WNBA stars: Napheesa Collier of the Minnesota Lynx and Breanna Stewart of the New York Liberty. Unrivaled was offering players an average salary of $220,000 for a ten-week season, roughly twice the WNBA

Chelsea celebrated winning her second Olympic gold medal in 2024 after Team USA defeated France.

average salary (approximately $120,000). Champions would collect an extra $50,000.

In that first season, Unrivaled featured six teams with three players to a side competing on a shorter indoor court than the WNBA's in one location—Miami. Chelsea felt like she was back playing pickup games in the Bay Area, whipping behind-the-back passes and pulling up for winning 3-pointers.

She wasn't the only one to thrive. While the players were on court for games or practices, Unrivaled offered full-time daycare for children. Lennox went from crawling in January to walking by March. Chelsea led her team (nicknamed the Rose Basketball Club) to the championship, where she was named MVP of the Finals.

After a few weeks of rest, Chelsea returned to the Las Vegas Aces for the 2025 WNBA season. It started shockingly poorly for the Aces, as they searched to find chemistry with the new additions to their team. At least Chelsea could take comfort in coming home to Lennox.

"That's her family, and you know what, it starts and ends there," her dad said. "With basketball at some point the bells and the whistles are gone, but you still have family."

After the Aces dropped to 14–14, losing by 53 points to the Minnesota Lynx on August 2, the Aces held a team meeting and determined enough was enough. They couldn't be embarrassed like that again. Together with superstar center A'ja Wilson, Chelsea and the other veterans tightened their defense, cut down on mistakes, and remembered what made them click as a team. At the time, Wilson had more assists per game than Chelsea. When Wilson told her that, Chelsea took it as motivation.

The Aces never lost another game to end their season, rattling off 16 straight victories.

"I wasn't playing to my potential," Chelsea said. "I was trying to prove so many things to myself and to prove people wrong that I was doing it in the wrong way."

So she went back to basics: "Just being me. Just being me got me to this point and it got me to my fourth ring."

Chelsea grabbed rebounds, sliced through defenses, and uplifted her teammates at every turn. Even her social media posts featured her teammates' performances before her own. Chelsea averaged 7.3 assists per game in the playoffs, a career high. She hit huge 3-pointers in the clutch throughout the postseason, including a pair in the fourth quarter of Game 4 of the WNBA finals against Phoenix that all but sealed the victory.

In the emotional celebration after, coach Becky Hammon embraced Chelsea. "What a lifesaver you are!" she told her point guard, caught on ESPN's microphone. "You're about winning. You're about all the right things."

Hammon has known that all along. It's why she can already see Chelsea's future in the game. "A coach or a general manager," she said, then joked: "She's already a coach on the floor. I'm like her assistant."

Chelsea still has goals as a player, and, of course, those goals don't just apply to her. The salaries and endorsement opportunities have increased since Chelsea entered the league, but she still has a vision of what women in pro basketball deserve:

"A seat at the table, and not just a seat at the table to fill a quota. A seat at the table because we're valued," said Chelsea, who was the player representative for the Las Vegas Aces negotiating for a new collective bargaining agreement. "Men still get paid more, men still have opportunities. And women are still judged a lot of times in the way they look and how they present themselves, rather than the work that they actually do."

More companies, she said, should invest in women's sports to grow the game so that it's no longer a novel thing. "What's crazy is that we're in 2025, and we're still like, this is the first Black something, this is the first woman to do this. And so, when you start limiting the number of times that you hear first, you're not breaking barriers anymore. It's normal now."

Chelsea's desire to treat others the way her family treated her is her gift. Her personal Instagram account posts her teammates' stat lines after games, pumping up their performances.

"She's a point guard in life," said her club coach, Quintero. "She wants everyone to be happy. And that selflessness is everywhere. I always see her treating everybody so well and joyfully. She wants to know about the other person, she never talks about herself. She wants to give, give, give."

For as long as she can, Chelsea will continue to put a special spin on her passes, a little something extra. Her ultimate goal?

"How can I make this game better than how I found it?" Chelsea said. "I want to be the teammate that everyone wants to join the fight with."

Naomi's crackling serve helped her reach the semifinals of the 2025 US Open at the USTA Billie Jean King National Tennis Center.

CHAPTER 11

NAOMI OSAKA, TENNIS

"KNOW YOUR HISTORY"

NO FANS WERE ALLOWED TO ATTEND LIVE SPORTING events in the COVID summer of 2020. For tennis players, that meant no roars in New York's Arthur Ashe Stadium, home to the biggest tournament on American soil, the US Open.

In this strange silence, though, one player made a ton of noise: Naomi Osaka.

A shy prodigy born in Japan to a Japanese mother and a Haitian-born father, Naomi had rocketed to the world's No. 1 ranking soon after beating Serena Williams in the 2018 US Open. Two years later, she used her newfound platform in a powerful way by single-handedly championing the cause of racial justice in the mostly white sport of tennis.

I'll never forget the climate in which athletes were playing that summer. When an unarmed Black man, George Floyd, was killed by a white police officer in Minnesota in May, his death touched off nationwide protests of police brutality that eventually spread around the globe. In August, when a Wisconsin police officer shot a Black man—Jacob Blake—seven times in the back, teams in the NBA and WNBA refused to play in protest.

In response to the shooting of Blake, Naomi announced on social media that she would not play her semifinal match at the Western & Southern Open, in protest of racial injustice: "As a Black woman," she wrote, "I feel like there are much more important matters at hand that need immediate attention, rather than watching me play tennis."

Instead of having Naomi forfeit the match, officials listened to her reasoning and paused the tournament for a day for all players.

Naomi was just getting warmed up. When the US Open started the next week, she brought seven different masks—each one bearing the name of a victim of police violence. She wore one mask each match, all the way to winning the 2020 championship.

When I look back to critical moments of sports and social activism, Naomi's stand puts her in the category of two other trailblazing Black tennis champions: Althea Gibson and Arthur Ashe.

Like Jackie Robinson in baseball, Gibson integrated the sport of tennis in 1950 when she became the first Black player to enter the US Nationals (what the US Open was called back then). Gibson would become the first Black player to win one of tennis's four major tournaments when she captured the French Open in 1956. She then won the US championships in 1957 and 1958; those same two years she also won Wimbledon.

(A little-known fact, Gibson also integrated the Ladies Professional Golf Association [LPGA] in 1963 when, at age 36, she started playing golf on the tour.)

Ashe is the only Black man to have won Wimbledon, the US Open, and the Australian Open.

My dear friend, Zina Garrison, who in 1990 became the first Black woman to reach the Wimbledon finals since Gibson, was amazed by Naomi's brave actions. She said that when Naomi wore the masks with the names of the seven victims, "She made an imprint, a very large imprint," Garrison said. "She changed sports."

By wearing those masks, Naomi sent a message to the world, but also a personal one to the family members of those victims. Deeply touched, they thanked her in interviews and on social media. Across the country, people cheered and cried over Naomi's US Open activism.

Garrison received text messages and phone calls from relatives and friends throughout the Black community. "I've never seen older Black people react the way they did," Garrison told me. "They were so proud that this girl took a stand. And you just don't see that in tennis."

Naomi's impact went far beyond the United States. In Japan, people embraced Naomi for her success and her sweet demeanor, and they were amazed by her political activism. By being such a charming champion in the public eye, she helped challenge Japan's long-held cultural beliefs that people of other races were inferior.

AS MY TENNIS FRIENDS IN JAPAN HAVE TOLD ME, it had not been accepted for a countryman to take a stand on political issues, let alone for an athlete. Or a woman. Or a biracial woman.

That took pure courage.

"I felt like I was suppressing my voice in not speaking up, and it was kind of building," Naomi told me. "And then I also just felt like I didn't really care if anyone judged me, because that's how I truly felt, and I had hoped that other people would feel the same way."

A year later, in May 2021, Naomi also took a stand at the French Open when the glare of the international media attention got too much to bear. She said she would not participate in post-match interviews, saying she wanted to protect her mental health.

Naomi was hurting. Perhaps she was unaware of the mental health support that the WTA has made available for its professional players since the late 1980s, support that officials keep confidential to respect players' privacy.

Of course, I recognize things are different today with the pressures of social media. I still think it is a responsibility for players at major tournaments to speak to the media who regularly follow tennis. French officials fined Naomi, saying interviews were part of an athlete's obligation. Naomi withdrew after winning her first-round match, announcing on social media that she had been struggling with depression since winning the 2018 US Open. She was taking a break from tennis.

In July 2021, she wrote an article for *Time* magazine titled, "It's O.K. Not to Be O.K.," about her mental health journey: "Believe it or not, I am naturally introverted and do not court the spotlight. I always try to push myself to speak up for what I believe to be right, but that often comes at a cost of great anxiety. I feel uncomfortable being the spokesperson or face of athlete mental health as it's still so new to me and I don't have all the answers. I do hope that people can relate and understand it's OK to not be OK, and it's OK to talk about it."

Her actions and words soon gave another superstar an

example to follow. During the pandemic-delayed Tokyo Olympics, held in July and August of 2021, the world's best gymnast, Simone Biles, was suddenly struck with her own mental health issues. Her mind and body were scarily out of sync mid-air, and she was unable to complete dangerous twists off the vault. Like Naomi, Simone announced she needed time off to clear her head. Naomi and Simone later privately messaged each other to offer support and gratitude, two mighty champions admitting vulnerability.

Tennis gave Naomi the platform to make a profound impact in 2020 and 2021, when she reached millions of followers worldwide on social media with her candid messages. I always tell athletes to "know their history." Naomi may not yet fully appreciate her place in history because she's still creating it.

"I guess people would see me and think that my life is amazing," Naomi told me. "But there's a lot of hard work that goes into that, and even then, the success isn't promised. Because there's so many hundreds of other people that are wanting to do the same thing as you."

NAOMI OSAKA WAS BORN IN OSAKA, JAPAN, IN October 1997, 18 months after her older sister, Mari. (It's a coincidence that their last name is the same as the name of their birth city.) At the time, the girls' parents, Tamaki Osaka and Leonard Maxime François, were running a clothing store.

Leonard was born in Haiti, moved to New York to attend college and then studied abroad in Japan where he met Tamaki. They fell in love. At first, Tamaki's parents did not approve of her marrying outside Japanese culture, and they shunned her. Tamaki and Leonard were on their own to raise two toddlers.

In 1999, Leonard turned on the television to see sisters Venus and Serena Williams win the French Open doubles title. It would be the first of the Williams' 14 Grand Slam doubles titles together. Knowing that their father had famously coached them early in their career, Leonard formed a plan with his wife.

"We were awestruck by Serena and Venus," Tamaki told the multilingual website, Nippon.com. "Here were two Black teenage sisters in a sport dominated by white players traveling the world, meeting different people, and experiencing new cultures. It was a life most girls their age could only fantasize about. I honestly felt that being a tennis player was a dream profession."

Leonard decided he would mold his daughters into the next Venus and Serena, coaching Mari and Naomi himself (without any training) like Richard Williams did for his daughters.

As Tamaki added in the website's article: "Seeing the Williams sisters took our minds off our struggles to make ends meet and started us dreaming a brighter future for our little girls. Our hopes were highest for Mari, who was very athletic even as a little girl."

Tamaki and Leonard began developing their daughters' athletic ability when they were toddlers. They had them chase a ball together in the park and challenged the girls to dangle from the bars on the jungle gym to tune their strength and hand-eye coordination.

Leonard decided the family should move to the US where they would have easier access to tennis courts. They stayed with his parents, who lived in Elmont on Long Island, ten minutes east of Queens in New York City.

Naomi was three years old when she started playing tennis. On the public tennis courts at Detective Keith L. Williams Park in Jamaica, Queens, Naomi and Mari hit thousands of

At just 16 years old and ranked No. 406 in the world, Naomi upset former US Open champion Samantha Stosur at the Bank of the West Classic tournament. It was a three-set thriller that put the world on notice.

balls with their father. The sisters were barely as tall as the net, yet they pounded the ball with a singular purpose: they were going to be champions.

In the summer, when the girls were around six and seven, they'd watch their elementary school classmates swim in the park's pool. Naomi and Mari would go to the other part of the park to play on the hard courts. In the fall, they returned to the courts after school—at least until they got kicked off to give someone else a turn.

"I remember I would watch other kids finish school, and they were able to go back home and do their homework and stuff like that," Naomi said. "And for me and my sister, we would go straight to the courts, and we would do our homework in the car."

Life for Naomi revolved around tennis. In third grade, she wrote a report about why Serena Williams was her favorite tennis player. By then, Serena had won seven Grand Slams tournaments.

At first, Naomi just wanted to win a game, then a set, and then a match off her older sister. For years, Naomi would lose 6-0, 6-0 virtually every time they played. Tennis players call the unfortunate "0" a "bagel." Nobody wants to get "bageled," especially by an older sibling.

"I was trying to beat my sister all the time, so that definitely fueled me," Naomi told me. "I do remember we used to bet, but it was kind of pointless to bet on tennis, because she was just so much better than me."

It would take her 12 years to finally beat Mari.

In 2006, Leonard decided that the family would move to Florida to escape the New York City winters and play on public courts year-round. He trained his daughters during the day in Pembroke Pines near Fort Lauderdale. They did school online at night.

"When I was 10, I honestly probably lived on the court," Naomi told me. "I definitely ate on the court and kind of slept on the court, too. I remember just always being at the tennis courts."

Leonard cycled through a series of professional coaches who were willing to coach his daughters when the family was unable to pay. Like she did on Long Island, Tamaki kept the family afloat by working nonstop. For a time, the family did not even have a dining room table in their small apartment and their refrigerator was often bare. Tamaki spoke about how poor they were back then in *Naomi Osaka: The Second Set*, a 2025 documentary film.

When Naomi was still a preteen, the coaches focused more on developing Mari's potential. Naomi then carried extra weight as she was growing into her tall frame.

But few people were observing their teen years. Since Richard Williams purposely kept Venus and Serena off the junior circuit—the traditional way young players break into the sport—Leonard did the same thing to preserve the mystery of his daughters' development. From the time they were 14 and allowed to turn pro, Mari and Naomi played mostly in entry-level tournaments on the International Tennis Federation (ITF) developmental circuit.

It was Naomi, and not Mari, who began showing more promise in those matches. At one stop in Alabama, Leonard set up a camera to film Naomi beating the French Open junior champion, Belinda Bencic. Naomi's crushing forehands became part of a 2013 video that Leonard created to attract sponsors for Naomi. At the end, he flashed through a series of childhood pictures of Naomi and Mari playing tennis.

"My goal is to become a tennis legend," Naomi says in a childlike voice in the video, which *Sports Illustrated* posted. "I'll do anything in my power to get there. So, I'll see you soon. Bye!"

She was right about "soon." In 2014, Naomi was 16 when she won two qualifying matches to get her into the main draw of a WTA tournament in Stanford, California. Naomi, who was then ranked No. 406 in the world, upset the 2011 US Open champion from Australia, Samantha Stosur, 4–6, 7–6 (7), 7–5 in the first round.

"It's probably the second-best win of my life," Osaka told reporters, "The first being when I first beat my sister."

- - - - ★ - - - - -

NAOMI LIVED A SHELTERED LIFE AS A TEENAGER, shuttling to tournaments across the southeastern states in a van with her parents and Mari. She never had sleepovers with friends like other "normal" teenagers. In the back seat, Naomi and Mari would draw (their fashion creations), do their homework, play video games, or just giggle together.

Naomi wanted to be a "legend," but she also had a more practical motivation for winning tennis matches: to make enough money to bring her family out of poverty. She especially wanted to help her mother.

"I just always really adored my mom, so wanting to make her life easier was always a really big goal of mine," she told me.

The family did receive financial assistance from the Japan Tennis Association to help afford training in Florida during Naomi's teenage years. It was fitting that it was in Japan where Naomi finally made it to the finals of her first WTA tournament: the Toray Pan Pacific Open in Tokyo in 2016. She lost to Caroline Wozniacki, 7–5, 6–3.

It is the longest-running women's tournament in Japan, and I won the tournament in its first year, 1973, beating Nancy Richey Gunter in the third set with a nifty drop shot. I believe that tournament inspired a new generation of Japanese tennis players to pick up the game in the late 1970s and 1980s.

With Naomi's runner-up finish in Tokyo in 2016, she lifted her world ranking to No. 40 and was named the WTA Newcomer of the Year. Naomi was still a bit raw as a player, but standing five-foot-eleven, she had all the tools of a star: a booming baseline forehand, a blistering serve, and blinding footspeed.

She was still waiting for her first title at the end of 2017 when she once again followed the path of her idol. Naomi hired Serena's former hitting partner, Sascha Bajin, as her new coach. She got results in March 2018, winning her first tournament at Indian Wells, California. Ranked No. 44 in the world at the time, Naomi upset world No. 1, Simona Halep, 6-3, 6-0, in the semifinals before cruising to the title.

Naomi gave her first on-court interview, nervously rambling and laughing as she kept forgetting what she wanted to say. She really hated public speaking. She preferred to let her 120 mph serves do the talking.

In the first round of the following tournament in Miami, she finally played Serena, who was returning to the court after 13 months of maternity leave. Naomi was nervous to play her longtime idol but still crushed her, 6–3, 6–2. Their next meeting would be even more memorable.

At 20 years old, Naomi entered the 2018 US Open ranked No. 19 in the world. She marched through the draw until she met Serena in the championship match. With Serena's career Grand Slam victory total stuck at 23, she was again attempting to tie Margaret Court's record of 24 Grand Slam wins.

That's when things got uncomfortable. Naomi cruised through the first set, with Serena's frustration growing. Early in the second set, the chair umpire Carlos Ramos from Portugal assessed Serena a code violation because he said she accepted help from her coach, Patrick Mouratoglou, who had been making hand gestures. Though the rule has since been changed to allow in-game coaching (since nearly every player was doing it anyway), Serena vehemently denied seeing any signals from her coach. She took it personally and told Ramos that.

That first violation was just a warning. Serena rode her emotions to a brief comeback, but when Naomi held strong, Serena smashed her racquet on the court. Ramos penalized her for unsportsmanlike conduct ("racquet abuse"). Because it was her second code violation, that resulted in a forfeited point. But Serena did not hear him in the roar of Arthur Ashe Stadium. The crowd was booing loudly. Meanwhile, Naomi was so rattled, she thought they were booing her and not the umpire.

When Serena realized she had been assessed a point penalty, she confronted Ramos again. He responded by giving her a third code violation, and that meant she forfeited a game. Naomi focused and won the match, 6–2, 6–4, to claim her first title at a major championship, known in tennis as a Grand Slam event. But everything felt a little off. She didn't jump up and down and celebrate. Instead, Naomi hugged Serena at the net. All during the trophy presentation, when the crowd was jeering loudly again in anger against Ramos, Naomi tugged at her visor to hide the tears falling down her face.

This wasn't how her first major victory was supposed to go, with vicious booing, whistling, and shouting from the crowd. Serena finally told the crowd to cheer for Naomi. She put her arm around her, consoling her.

Naomi's life would never be the same.

IN 2019, NAOMI BESTED SERENA IN ANOTHER category: She became the highest paid female athlete in the world, with $37.4 million in endorsements and prize money, according to *Forbes* magazine.

A year later, Naomi broke that record by earning $55.2 million according to the sports business news outlet, *Sportico*. Sponsors in both Japan and the US could see how she connected with millions of fans with her candid and self-effacing personality. But that year, Naomi's message also turned serious.

As she said in *Naomi Osaka: The Second Set*, the Netflix documentary she produced, Naomi felt like she had always been following other people's blueprints—Serena's especially. But when tennis came to a standstill because of COVID, Naomi finally had time to reflect. She wanted to chart her own path, this time as a leader.

When people protested in the streets of Minneapolis, Minnesota, where police had fatally held down George Floyd while arresting him, Naomi wanted to go there. She and her then-boyfriend, the rapper Cordae Dunston, flew in a private plane from Los Angeles (where Naomi was living) to march and take video alongside other protestors.

On July 1, 2020, Naomi wrote a powerful opinion piece in *Esquire* magazine calling out the injustice of police brutality and systemic racism.

"Black people have been fighting this oppression alone for so many years and progress has been fleeting at best," she wrote. "Being 'not racist' is not enough. We have to be anti-racist."

This was remarkable considering just how conservative

the tennis establishment had always been. The last time a tennis player wrote such an important opinion piece on race was in 1950. That's when Alice Marble (my former coach) wrote in *American Lawn Tennis* magazine urging tennis's all-white officials to end their discriminatory practices and let Althea Gibson play in the US Nationals. Later that summer, they did.

Naomi was sharpening her voice as well as her strokes. Even though COVID was still raging in the summer of 2020, the professional tennis season resumed cautiously without fans in August with the Western & Southern Open. That tournament usually is held in Cincinnati, but officials agreed to move it to the same courts as the US Open in New York. That way, the vaccinated players would be in a bubble for back-to-back tournaments, concluding with the US Open.

As with other US pro sports leagues at the time—men's and women's basketball, especially—the athletes took stands to protest recent violent incidents against Black people. Naomi said she would withdraw from the tournament in protest. Instead, her stand led the Western & Southern Open to suspend play for a day for everyone.

Ever humble, Naomi said she was surprised that her voice carried so much weight. She thought only established legends like Roger Federer, Rafael Nadal, or Serena Williams would have the power to stop a tournament.

"I don't feel like I'm being brave," Naomi told reporters. "I just feel like I'm doing what I should be doing."

When the tournament resumed, Naomi won that semifinal match but then pulled out of the tournament with a hamstring injury before the final against Victoria Azarenka. She did not want to risk worsening the injury before the US Open.

The Open began a week later on those same courts,

which I'm humbled tennis officials renamed for me in 2006: The USTA Billie Jean King National Tennis Center.

After the US Open, the 22 outdoor courts and 12 indoor courts at the Center in Flushing, New York (in the borough of Queens) are open to the public, year-round. As I always say: "Mi casa es su casa."

For her first match of the 2020 US Open, Naomi walked out with her hamstring wrapped, her trademark headphones playing psych-up music, and a black cloth mask with white lettering.

Each time she won another match, Naomi would put the mask back on for her on-court interview so that people would remember or learn about Black victims of violence and racial injustice: **Breonna Taylor** (shot and killed by police during a raid of her apartment in Louisville, Kentucky, in March 2020); **Elijah McClain** (police officers in Aurora, Colorado put him

Naomi won her second US Open title in 2020 at the height of the COVID pandemic, wearing face masks bearing the names of Black victims of police violence and racial profiling.

in a fatal chokehold in 2019); **Ahmaud Arbery** (jogging in Georgia in February 2020, he was chased by two men who shot him and another who filmed it); **Trayvon Martin** (a 17-year-old returning from a convenience store was shot and killed by a neighborhood watch volunteer in Florida in 2012); **George Floyd** (restrained, fatally, by a Minneapolis police officer); **Philando Castile** (shot and killed during a suburban St. Paul, Minnesota, police traffic stop in 2016).

When Naomi met Azarenka in the singles championship, she walked out wearing the black mask with "**Tamir Rice**" in white letters (Rice was 12 years old when he was shot and killed by a police officer in Cleveland while holding what was a toy pistol in 2014). After Naomi beat Azarenka in three sets, she lay on her back looking up at an empty Arthur Ashe Stadium, soaking in the echoes of history.

When asked by ESPN reporter Tom Rinaldi on court what message she was trying to send with the masks, Naomi quickly countered: "Well, what was the message that YOU got is more the question."

And then she went on. "I feel like the point is to make people start talking."

BACK IN JAPAN, WHERE Naomi had already become a celebrity, her activism was met with curiosity and even criticism. It just wasn't normal to speak out as an individual. But Kimiko Date, the biggest women's tennis star from Japan during the 1990s, was impressed with Naomi's boldness amid such international attention.

"From my personal perspective, in Japan, it's generally not welcomed when athletes get involved in social or political issues," Date told me in a WhatsApp exchange. "At any point in time, there are risks involved when someone takes a bold stance or speaks out, and with that comes a certain responsibility. I feel that this may have been the moment when Naomi herself began to express her own thoughts and beliefs through her actions and words."

Date, who had risen as high as No. 4 in the world in 1995 before her first retirement the following year, said in the rare times when she did speak about social issues, the media would criticize her. "I personally experienced many painful moments because of this," she told me. "That's why I deeply respect Naomi's courage in using her voice."

But even Naomi admitted it had not been easy. In the *Esquire* piece from 2020, Naomi addressed the racism that Black people felt in Japan. Because she is biracial, she is known by the Japanese term *hafu*—or half.

"Japan is a very homogenous country, so tackling racism has been challenging for me," she wrote. "I have received racist comments online and even on TV. But that's the minority. In reality, biracial people—especially biracial athletes—are the future of Japan."

She felt that she and other Black and Japanese athletes—including NBA forward Rui Hachimura—were "embraced by the majority of the public, fans, sponsors, and media."

She added: "We can't let the ignorance of a few hold back the progressiveness of the masses. The love I feel from Japanese fans of all ages, especially the younger ones, has always been heartwarming. I am so proud to represent Japan and always will be."

Naomi had been representing Japan since she was a teenager to honor the tennis federation's financial commitment to her, even though she makes her home in the US.

Just before her twenty-second birthday, in 2019, Naomi

"The love I feel from Japanese fans of all ages, especially the younger ones, has always been heartwarming."

Fans in her native Japan adore Naomi, who was born in Osaka, and competes for Japan.

had to make a life-changing decision. Japanese law requires that to be a Japanese citizen after age 22, one must give up any other citizenship. Naomi chose to give up her US citizenship.

When Naomi first came into her tennis stardom, she was not fluent in Japanese. But she understood it and did her best to answer reporters' questions after matches—often in English. Stories about her in Japan tended to feature Naomi away from sports, like highlighting her fashion choices and her off-court charity work. In 2020, she founded PLAY Academy in Japan to give opportunities in sports to girls from underserved communities.

In that respect, Naomi is following a tradition established by former pros like Kimiko Date who, in 2019, launched her own program for junior girls to grow the game in Japan.

"Spending time with these junior players, one clear change I've noticed is that winning a Grand Slam is no longer seen as just a dream—it's become a tangible goal," Date told me. "Today's juniors have seen Naomi Osaka lift Grand Slam trophies with their own eyes. That visual impact is incredibly powerful."

At the 2021 Tokyo Summer Olympics, Japan's Olympic federation gave Naomi the highest honor: lighting the cauldron during the Olympic opening ceremony signifying that the Games were formally underway. That privilege put Naomi on par with the legendary boxer Muhammad Ali, who lit the flame at the 1996 Atlanta Games.

Naomi later said she was just trying not to fall while walking to the top of the stadium. She came to understand what the image of her lighting the torch projected for other biracial people in Japan. "I heard that there were a lot of mixed kids—and mixed grownups as well—who were really touched and moved by it," she told me.

Naomi knows she carries many identities at once, from living in New York, then Florida, and now in California, to representing Japan, to funding a tennis academy in her father's homeland of Haiti. She feels very connected to her Japanese heritage.

"I feel like Japanese culture is ingrained in my day-to-day life so there's not a time where I don't feel Japanese," she told *The Japan Times* in 2025. "The food I eat, the clothes I wear and even my reserved personality—it all traces back to Japan. In every city I travel to, I typically make a point to find good Japanese food as that makes me feel most at home."

Naomi can be gracious on the court, a trait that would seem to clash with being a ruthless champion in a solo sport. I've seen her bow to her opponent before warm-ups. Then she pummels the ball.

In the 2019 third round of the US Open, Naomi handily beat Coco Gauff—who was then fifteen years old and making her Open debut. Naomi saw Coco crying in her chair afterward, so she walked over and asked Coco to join her for the on-court interview. When it was Naomi's turn to speak, she took the microphone, turned to Coco's parents in the stands, and said, "You guys raised an amazing player."

Her generous personality comes out in other ways. During the first round of the Bad Homburg tournament in Germany in June 2025, Naomi was coming back in the second set against American Emma Navarro. Naomi hit a forehand errantly and thought it was going out. She groaned loudly before the ball bounced in. Navarro hit the ball into the net.

It is an obscure tennis rule that players cannot talk while a point is still being played so they don't disrupt the action. (Grunting or even shrieking apparently does not count as actual talking.) Navarro did not complain, but Naomi reported herself to the chair umpire. The umpire accepted the admission and awarded the point to Navarro. Naomi went on to lose the match, but coaches and tennis players applauded her sportsmanship.

AT THE BEGINNING OF 2023, NAOMI ANNOUNCED that she was expecting a baby that summer, and that she was taking another break from tennis. In July, she gave birth to her daughter, Shai.

Meanwhile, other Black athletes stepped into the spotlight to win major tournaments: Coco Gauff (2023 US Open, 2025 French Open) and Madison Keys (2025 Australian Open). Naomi was in the crowd at the 2023 Open, two months after giving birth to Shai, to watch Coco. But she was also dreaming of how soon she could return to the court.

It took longer than she thought. In 2024, Naomi struggled to find the same level of success that she had in 2020 and 2021. She hired and then fired two high-profile coaches. Her father still advised Naomi on her career but, as had been his routine, was too nervous to watch her matches from her players' box. Her mother was a constant presence.

Her sister, Mari, was now a fashion designer, having retired from tennis in 2021 after topping out at No. 281 in the world rankings. Mari said on social media that her pro career was a journey that she "ultimately did not enjoy."

For a while, it looked like Naomi was not enjoying the game either, as she impatiently judged her success against other players who had come back after giving birth. But those closest to her knew that once she became healthy again—she had strained her abdominal muscle at the end of

2024, and it reoccurred during the 2025 Australian Open—Naomi would be back among the world's best.

At the end of July 2025, Naomi started working with Polish coach Tomasz Wiktorowski (who previously coached former No. 1 Iga Świątek). Naomi played with renewed spirit and got immediate results from the partnership with Wiktorowski. In her first tournament with him, she made the finals of the Canadian Open in Montreal before losing to Canadian teenager, Victoria Mboko.

When she got to New York for the 2025 US Open, she brought a sense of perspective which she shared with reporters. "Honestly since I've come back, I kind of wanted everything to happen really quickly," she said to the media. "Sometimes I think about me before I had my pregnancy break. And I feel like my age was pretty young when I was doing the stuff I was doing, and I feel like I have to give myself grace on that."

Beyond this display of calm, Naomi brought something else new to her game: the summer's hottest good luck charm, the Labubu. A collectible plush elf-like doll with pointy ears and a mischievous grin created by Hong Kong-born illustrator Kasing Lung—and produced by Chinese toy company Pop Mart—the figurine usually dangles from purses or bags. Naomi wanted to put her own spin on it, and enlisted New York artist Kerin Rose Gold to create a custom figurine with colored sparkling crystals, complete with a tennis racquet. Billie Jean Bling was born.

Naomi lifted the bag with the Labubu during her on-court interview after her first-round victory. When she announced the clever name she had given it, the crowd roared in appreciation. Naomi at first intended the figurine to be an accessory for the sparkly Nike tennis outfit she designed, matching the crystal roses the artist also made for her hair. But, in that moment, Billie Jean Bling became an instant sensation.

I got such a kick out of it that my team contacted Gold to see if I could get a replica. The New York artist ended up making a second Labubu for me that had my signature red-framed glasses; Naomi named her LaBillieBu, as she told the crowd after her second-round win. Got to love it!

Naomi posed with my Labubu namesake: "Billie Jean Bling." Naomi turned the trend into a sensation with her different tennis-themed bejeweled figurines during the 2025 US Open.

Although other players attached fuzzy Labubus to their tennis bags, no one owned the trend like Naomi that US Open. She launched one doll for each match, with shiny puns on the names of tennis legends: Arthur Flashe (after Arthur Ashe), Althea Glitterson (Althea Gibson), Andre Swagassi (Andre Agassi), and John McEnglow (John McEnroe).

Of course, we will remember Naomi's run to the semifinal of the 2025 US Open for more than just her fashion choices. But they were a sign that she was playing with joy again, and that she was comfortable designing her own role in the spotlight. Her much-improved fitness allowed her to get into position to hit sizzling forehand winners and control points. She was confident again, even smiling. She knew she had put in the work to return to this point.

In the 2025 US Open's fourth round, she crushed Coco Gauff, much like she did back in 2019. In the quarterfinals match against Czech star, Karolína Muchová, Naomi defeated her in straight sets which led her to share this revelation:

"I learned I love tennis way more than I thought I did," Naomi told reporters after the quarterfinals win. "And I learned that, you know, I actually really love challenges. It's like a video game. You pick it up, and even if you lose a level, you kind of just restart and keep going until you eventually win. And I think it's a little tough at some times, but I wouldn't trade it for the world."

In the semifinals against American Amanda Anisimova, Naomi faced a 24-year-old power player who, like her, had also taken a mental health break from tennis. Naomi battled Anisimova past midnight, winning the first set in a tiebreak, losing the second set in a tiebreak, and then fell in the third set.

"Honestly, I don't feel sad. I feel like I did the best I could," Naomi told the media. "It's kind of inspiring for me because it makes me want to train and try to get better."

Naomi insisted the only regret she had was not being able to debut a seventh Labubu for the final. That one was going to be herself—modeled after her favorite lime green outfit she designed for the 2024 US Open, complete with a big white bow on the back.

"That's the worst thing," Naomi said, half-jokingly. "I'm fine losing, but don't ask me about this Labubu."

ACKNOWLEDGMENTS

THIS BOOK WOULD NOT HAVE BEEN POSSIBLE without Ilana Kloss, my life partner, business partner, and chief executive of Billie Jean King Enterprises. As I say in our chapter chronicling hockey player, Kendall Coyne Schofield, "I dream it, and Ilana builds it." Here, Ilana immediately saw the potential of this book to inspire a young adult audience. She pushed it along at every stage. She knew how important it was to me to teach the next generation and provide teens with a top team of trailblazers for role models. Ilana grew up in South Africa, where she not only became a professional tennis player, but she also developed a passion for social justice that we share. We're not finished trying to change the world.

Ilana was with me when, during the 2025 United States Open, my dear brother, Randy Moffitt passed away at age 76 after a long illness. We had made many trips to California to be with him in the past several years, and I know I did all I could to make that precious time. Still, I am devastated to have lost my teammate, my first champion, and my fellow professional athlete. We did everything together as kids before we started developing our careers. Randy was a relief pitcher who played 12 seasons in Major League Baseball, 10 for the San Francisco Giants, one season with the Houston

Astros, and one with the Toronto Blue Jays. I had begged for my parents to give me a younger sibling, and when they did, I had my own family nickname: "Sis."

Writing this book made me appreciate the role that siblings play in the development of an athlete. They push us, keep us real, and keep us laughing. I know I am honoring my brother's legacy by chronicling the relationships these 11 athletes had with their younger and older siblings. I will forever cherish our years of playing baseball in the yard together. May every young person be so lucky to have a brother like Randy.

My parents, Bill and Betty Moffitt, supported my love for sports and my desire to be No. 1 in the world from the time I was 11. They were devoted in a way that was unusual in the 1950s and 1960s, even as it seems natural today. We would like to thank the parents of the athletes in this book for their dedication, not to mention all the hundreds of thousands of miles they (collectively) put on their beat-up minivans and pickup trucks schlepping their kids around the country to tournaments. Their words reminded me that most parents do not intend to raise a trailblazer, but their unconditional support helps make it happen. Thank you to Teresa Coan, Ahlise Coyne, Elana Elor, Jaime Flores, Vickey and James Gray, Liz and Tom Hiltz, Jermaine and Mesha O'Neal, James Purce, and Scott Whitmore. With patience, grace, and good humor you spoke to us often more than once, and were available for follow-up interviews on your favorite subject.

Your family is your first team in life, your forever team. My work team at Billie Jean King Enterprises is my everyday family. Thank you to Marjorie Gantman for reading early chapters and for your nonstop support. Kristi Gaylord, social media expert, Josh Blackman for reviewing photos, Therese O'Higgins and Andrew Doran for all-around excellence, and

Barbara Perry for all your work with our athletes. Tip Nunn, my longtime publicist and dear friend, promotes my passions while somehow organizing my schedule. I trust his guidance without hesitation.

I am very grateful to David Black and Joy Tutela, my literary agents who worked tirelessly to find the right home for this unique book. Thanks also to Anna Zinchuk and Nell Beck at the David Black Agency for helping make an All-Star team.

We would like to thank Carolyn Yoder, the editorial director of Calkins Creek, an imprint of Astra Books for Young Readers. A lifelong children's book editor, Carolyn first saw the potential to inspire a new generation of humans, not just athletes, to accomplish great things. Thalia Leaf made the words come to life by securing photographs, and when she left for maternity leave, Julia Block carried on her work at Calkins Creek.

Today, sports agents play a critical role in managing the outside projects for their athletes. Thank you to these agents:

Alan Zucker at Excel Sports, who worked with Caitlin Clark's primary agent Erin Kane, along with Collen Garrity to secure Caitlin's participation; Stuart Duguid, Naomi Osaka's longtime agent; Ciara Billups, Chantal Romain, and Jade-Li English at KLUTCH Sports who represent Chelsea Gray; Merhawi Keflezighi has quality human beings on his track and field team, from his brother, marathon champion Meb Keflezighi, to 1,500-meter star, Nikki Hiltz; working with Diana Flores, SMAC Entertainment's Constance Schwartz-Morini, Jose Diaz, and Marchella Gigliotti understood the concept of the book from the very beginning; Deddrick Faison and Hal Biagas at Valor Sports Agency, who win the award for the most responsive agents in the business. Their partner and co-founder of Valor Sports Agency, the retired NBA All-Star Jermaine O'Neal, was incredibly gracious in talking about his daughter, Asjia O'Neal. Maicy (MJ) Schwartz at Offseason Productions, Midge Purce's assistant and liaison, patiently tracked down facts from an always-on-the-go Midge. Barbara Perry, Kendall Coyne Schofield's agent, has seen it all in this business and translates those lessons to success.

I have long believed that sports media relations directors are the background stars of the game. They are true professionals, and we would like to thank them for their indispensable help: Joe Anderson of the Minnesota Frost of the Professional Women's Hockey League (PWHL), along with Mandy Gutmann, Vice President of Communications and External Affairs for the PWHL. Caroline Williams at the Las Vegas Aces of the Women's National Basketball Association (WNBA), who has been in the game from the beginning when she directed media for USA Basketball. Caroline understands the journey. Morgan Randolph at the Golden State Valkyries found a spot on press row for a veteran reporter, as did Bryan Flannery at the New York Liberty. Gary Abbott at USA Wrestling is a legend for all Olympic PR people and has been talking about women's wrestling for decades. Kristen Gowdy at the United States Olympic and Paralympic Committee suggested quite correctly that we speak to McKenzie Coan at the 2024 Olympic Media Summit in New York to ask about her participation in the book. (McKenzie's reaction: "Yes! Oh my God, yes!") Olivia Truby at USA Para Swimming provided wonderful photos. Jeff Greer at Gotham FC of the National Women's Soccer League, a former journalist, understood what we needed and worked diligently to get it. Cathy Jerome and Sam Pittman at the Washington Spirit were welcoming, and Zuhayr Muang at the Utah Royals was immediately helpful. Anthony Baldini, founder of Athlete Strategies, secured interviews and answers. Natalie Mikolich offered timely help at the WPBL. On the college level, many thanks to Ashleigh Young, John Bianco, and Jeremy Rosenthal at the University of Texas, and Bailey Turner at the University of Iowa.

In 2023, Liz Robbins approached me because she was writing a 50th anniversary piece about 1973, the year I helped bring about pay equity at the US Open. That was also the year I founded the Women's Tennis Association. Writing first for *The New York Times International* edition, Liz captured my equity efforts in the past, but also what I have been doing in the present to create opportunities for women in professional sports. We later spoke about how the seeds of leadership are sowed in an athlete's teen years. What better way to promote sports, reading, and dreaming than to write a book for young adults. This is the book Liz wished she had when she was a high school athlete growing up in the 1980s in Philadelphia. I'll let Liz do some acknowledging here:

I would like to thank my husband, Ricardo Reif for his patience, support, and for shouting out the T-shirt slogan, "Everyone Watches Women's Sports," whenever the television was tuned to a game. He provided Spanish translation on a Zoom interview with Diana Flores's father, Jaime. Carl Nelson, a longtime deputy sports editor at *The New York Times* and word wizard, edited with his trademark blend of care and honesty. Even now, away from nightly deadlines, I rely on him. Former deputy media editor at *The Times* and now executive editor at *The Trace*, Craig Hunter, offered invaluable perspective and support. Lori Shontz, professor of practice at the University of Oregon's School of Journalism and Communication, and my dear friend since we covered the 1995 NCAA Women's Final Four and track and field at the 1996 Atlanta Olympics together, reviewed the Nikki Hiltz and Caitlin Clark chapters. Julia Schwalb, who directed the compelling film *Kick* on Nikki, shared an early excerpt with us. Hannah Wunsch, hockey player, doctor, playwright and author, offered a keen eye on Kendall Coyne Schofield's chapter. Jim Sterngold, longtime *Wall Street Journal* and *New York Times* journalist, and contributing author, himself, offered wisdom and reassurance. Thanks to Laura Kent, my tennis partner and unofficial doctor, for Friday hits on the Hudson. And to Michael Gately, Executive Director of Biographers International Organization, for boosting me and the craft. Big hugs to my nieces and soccer stars, Liat and Samara, for providing helpful teenage insight.

Profound thanks to Wendy Robbins, my mom, and the late Larry Robbins, my dad, for raising a writer, athlete, and sports fan in Philadelphia. In March 2024, my mom and I went to the Albany regional NCAA women's basketball tournament. In a sold-out arena, we witnessed the growth of women's basketball firsthand. We got to see the eventual champion South Carolina Gamecocks expertly win their Sweet 16 game, coached by Philadelphia's own Dawn Staley. Staley's journey from high school legend to the Basketball Hall of Fame blazed a trail for generations to come.

We hope this book inspires you to be that next generation. That's why we chronicle those athletes you may already know and those we think you should know in this new era of women's sports. Finally, we thank these 11 extraordinary leaders for being so honest with us and with you.

BIBLIOGRAPHY AND SOURCE NOTES

Quotations in each chapter are from personal interviews or from sources marked with an asterisk (*).

CHAPTER 1

CAITLIN CLARK, BASKETBALL "PRESSURE IS A PRIVILEGE"

Personal interviews:
Caitlin Clark
Lisa Bluder
Kristin Meyer
Dickson Jensen

*Boyd, James. "Caitlin Clark says Bigotry Has 'No Place' in WNBA Amid Probe into Fans' Alleged Hate Comments," *The Athletic*. May 19, 2025, nytimes.com/athletic/6368634/2025/05/19/caitlin-clark-comments-wnba-investigation-angel-reese-hateful-comments.

*Gregory, Sean. "Caitlin Clark: Athlete of the Year," *Time*, Dec. 10, 2024, time.com/7200904/athlete-of-the-year-2024-caitlin-clark/.

Harty, Pat. "A Look Back When 5-year-old Caitlin Clark Stood Up to, and Stood Over a Bully." *Hawk Fanatic*, March 27, 2023, hawkfanatic.com/2023/03/27/a-look-back-at-when-five-year-old-caitlin-clark-stood-up-to-and-stood-over-a-bully/.

*Leistikow, Chad. "Why Iowa basketball's Caitlin Clark could have been a superstar in soccer, too." *Des Moines Register*, Feb. 8, 2024, hawkcentral.com/story/sports/college/iowa/basketball-women/2024/02/08/iowa-womens-basketball-caitlin-clark-ncaa-scoring-record-soccer dowling-catholic-ncaa/72339992007/.

Robbins, Liz. "A Stunning Year in Sports: Caitlin Clark, Shohei Ohtani and Record Viewership." *New York Times*, Dec. 13, 2024, nytimes.com/2024/12/13/sports/caitlin-clark-best-year.html.

*Dawn Staley Award website. "Caitlin Clark Named the 2023 Dawn Staley Award Winner: Caitlin is the First Three-Time Winner of the Award." April 6, 2023, dawnstaleyaward.org/home-2024-clark#:~:text=The%20Phoenix%20Club%20of%20Philadelphia,and%20her%20will%20to%20win.

Thompson, Wright. "Caitlin Clark and Iowa Find Peace in the Process." *ESPN*, March 20, 2024, espn.com/womens-college-basketball/story/_/id/39740282/caitlin-clark-iowa-2024-ncaa-women-basketball-tournament-ready-march.

*TikTok account @lexmadee. "Why do you wear No. 22?" tiktok.com/@lexmadee/video/7462920955531103530.

Villa, Walter. "After a Measured Approach to Trials, Recruit Clark Riding High with USA Basketball." *ESPN*, May 30, 2017, espn.com/espnw/sports/story/_/id/19577932/dowling-catholic-caitlin-clark-rides-athleticism-usa-basketball-roster-spot-fiba-americas-argentina.

CHAPTER 2

DIANA FLORES, FLAG FOOTBALL "YOU HAVE TO SEE IT TO BE IT"

Personal interviews:
Diana Flores
Jaime Flores (Sr.) and Jaime (Jr).
Jeff Reimel
Mike Reimel
Sam Rapoport

**Good Game with Sarah Spain*. IHeart Radio network. Sept. 1, 2025, iheart.com/podcast/1119-good-game-with-sarah-spai-185664375/episode/piensa-en-oro-with-diana-flores-291445522/.

CHAPTER 3

KENDALL COYNE SCHOFIELD, ICE HOCKEY "ASK FOR WHAT YOU WANT AND WHAT YOU NEED"

Personal interviews:
Kendall Coyne Schofield
Ahlise Coyne
Kevin Coyne
Manon Rhéaume
Ilana Kloss
Jayna Hefford
Nicole Hensley
Larry Pedrie

Coyne, Kendall. *As Fast as Her*. With Estelle Laure. Zondervan, 2022.

Shmerler, Cindy. "A Hockey Player Wanted to Form a Pro League. Billie Jean King Made it Happen." *New York Times*, Aug. 14, 2024, nytimes.com/2024/08/13/sports/hockey/womens-hockey-league-billie-jean-king.html.

CHAPTER 4

MIDGE PURCE, SOCCER "RELATIONSHIPS ARE EVERYTHING"

Personal interviews:
Midge Purce
James Purce
Jim Bruno
Imani Dorsey

*Bushnell, Henry. "Megan Rapinoe Meets with President Biden on Equal Pay Day: 'I've been devalued . . . because I am a woman.'" *Yahoo Sports*, March 24, 2021, sports.yahoo.com/megan-rapinoe-congress-equal-pay-white-house-180132827.html.

Dilts, A. J. "Margaret Purce '17: Prolific Goal Setter, Scorer, and Achiever." *Harvard Crimson*, May 27, 2021, thecrimson.com/article/2021/5/27/Purce-Feature/.

———. “Raising a Harvard Graduate and Soccer Star! Midge Purce and her Father Join Kickin’ It.” *Attacking Third.* YouTube, Nov. 24, 2023, youtube.com/watch?v=k9Qsl1HJgac.

Katie Nolan and Midge Purce. “The NWSL, Spicy Fiction, and Harvard Dorm Parties, with Midge Purce.” *Casuals* podcast, March 27, 2025, iheart.com/podcast/269-casuals-with-katie-nolan-255227604/episode/the-nwsl-spicy-fiction-and-harvard-271140560/.

“Purce ’17 Elected to Harvard Board of Overseers.” Harvard University, Aug. 21, 2020, gocrimson.com/news/2020/8/21/womens-soccer-purce-17-elected-to-harvard-board-of-overseers.aspx.

Tannenwald, David L. “Foot, Ball, Goal: Harvard Soccer Star Margaret ‘Midge’ Purce Featured.” *Harvard Magazine*, June 16, 2015, harvardmagazine.com/2015/06/foot-ball-goal.

*“World Cup Final Preview with Alyssa Thompson & Ali Riley.” *91st Minute podcast, Katie Nolan and Midge Purce, Just Women’s Sports*, Aug. 17, 2023, youtube.com/watch?v=gWbcC7qev4U&t=116s.

CHAPTER 5

ASJIA O'NEAL, VOLLEYBALL "PERSPECTIVE IS PRICELESS"

Personal interviews:
Asjia O’Neal
Jermaine O’Neal
Mesha O’Neal
Jerritt Elliott
Alina Lam

Kumar, Aishwarya. “The Extraordinary Courage of NCAA Volleyball Star Asjia O’Neal.” *ESPN*, Dec. 3, 2021, espn.com/college-sports/story/_/id/32697350/the-extraordinary-courage-ncaa-volleyball-star-asjia-oneal.

O’Neal, Asjia. “Started from the Bottom.” *The Players’ Tribune*, Jan. 4, 2024, theplayerstribune.com/posts/asjia-oneal-texas-longhorns-ncaa-college-volleyball.

*Logan Eggelston and Asjia O'Neal. "Roomie Diaries: Episode 2." YouTube, League One Volleyball, June 2025, youtube.com/watch?v=8o3eaYe5d_w.

CHAPTER 6

KELSIE WHITMORE, BASEBALL "YOU DEFINE YOURSELF"

Personal interviews:
Kelsie Whitmore
Scott Whitmore
Matthew Whitmore
Kelly Ford
Justine Siegal

Arrey, Taylor. "A Titan Takes the Field." *Titan Magazine*, Digital Magazine of Cal State Fullerton. Spring/Summer 2023, titanmag.fullerton.edu/spring-summer-2023/titan-in-the-outfield/.

Craig, Mary. "Vassar and Beyond: Women in Baseball in the 1800s," SB Nation, Beyond the Box Score, Sept. 19, 2017, beyondtheboxscore.com/2017/9/19/16323942/women-baseball-history-vassar-suffrage-abolition.

Fruth, Jean, dir. *See Her Be Her*. 2024; *Grassroots Baseball*. Amazon Prime.

*Instagram account, @Kelsie_Whitmore: instagram.com/reel/DOeu7m9iT9s/?utm_source=ig_web_copy_link&igsh=Z3Nqb2ZxM280MHp3.

*"Kelsie Whitmore: Men's Professional Baseball's Only Woman Player." *Grassroots Baseball*, YouTube. Oct. 13, 2022, youtube.com/watch?v=0g0DgjpJFIY.

Megdal, Howard. "Exclusive: Kelsie Whitmore joins the WPBL." *The IX Sports*, July 9, 2025, theixsports.com/features/exclusive-kelsie-whitmore-joins-the-wpbl/.

Maddox, Callie. "Women are Reclaiming Their Place in Baseball." *The Conversation*, March 27, 2025, theconversation.com/women-are-reclaiming-their-place-in-baseball-252590?utm_source=substack&utm_medium=email.

Schonbrun, Zach. "Always an Outlier, Kelsie Whitmore Just Wants to Play Baseball." *New York Times*, June 12, 2022, nytimes.com/2022/06/12/sports/baseball/kelsie-whitmore-staten-island.html.

Stompers Baseball. "Francis Ford Coppola and Sonoma Stompers Promote Recruitment, Development and Advancement of Women in Baseball." June 27, 2016, stompersbaseball.com/news/2016/6/27/francis-ford-coppola-and-sonoma-stompers-promote-recruitment-development-and-advancement-of-women-in-baseball.

Weber, Bruce. "Judge Sylvia Pressler, Who Opened Little League to Girls, Dies at 75." *New York Times*, Feb. 17, 2010, nytimes.com/2010/02/17/nyregion/17pressler.html.

"Women in Baseball." National Baseball Hall of Fame. baseballhall.org/women-in-baseball.

CHAPTER 7

AMIT ELOR, WRESTLING "BE A PROBLEM SOLVER"

Personal interviews:
Amit Elor
Elana Elor
Orry Elor
Ronny Elor
Sara McMann
Terry Steiner

Berg, Aimee. "Facing family tragedy, online antisemitism, US wrestler Amit Elor vies for gold in Paris." *Times of Israel*, Aug. 5, 2024, timesofisrael.com/facing-family-tragedy-online-antisemitism-us-wrestler-amit-elor-vies-for-gold-in-paris/.

Gartrell, Nate. "Jury Convicts Two in Pleasant Hill shooting." *Mercury News*, Jan. 15, 2020.

*Instagram account @amitelor1, instagram.com/amitelor1/.

NBC Bay Area. "Wrestling Gold Medalist Amit Elor on Finding Resilience After Tragedy: Anything Hard in Life Makes You Stronger." Aug. 7, 2024. nbcbayarea.com/video/paris-2024-summer-olympics/wrestling-gold-medalist-amit-elor-on-finding-resilience-after-tragedy-anything-hard-in-life-makes-you-stronger/3617895/.

CHAPTER 8

McKENZIE COAN, SWIMMING "CELEBRATE OUR DIFFERENCES"

Personal interviews:
McKenzie Coan
Teresa Coan
Grant Coan
Kara Ayers

Coan, McKenzie. *Breaking Free: Shattering Expectations and Thriving with Ambition in Pursuit of Gold*. With Holly Neumann. CG Sports Publishing, 2021.

"Coan Returns to Loyola a Gold Medal Champion." *Loyola Greyhounds News*, Oct. 25, 2016, loyolagreyhounds.com/news/2016/10/25/Coan_Returns_To_Loyola_A_Gold_Medal_Champion.aspx.

Pringle, Eleanor. "Some Paralympic athletes will receive 75% less than their Olympic peers for winning a gold medal." *Fortune*, Sept. 2, 2024, fortune.com/2024/09/02/paralympic-athletes-payment-prize-parity-olympic-medalists/.

CHAPTER 9

NIKKI HILTZ, TRACK "CHAMPIONS ADJUST"

Personal interviews:
Nikki Hiltz
Michaela Hiltz
Liz Hiltz
Tom Hiltz
Emma Gee
Dan Gruber

Culp, Jennifer. “Nikki Hiltz is Blazing a Trail.” June 6, 2023, *Them Magazine*, them.us/story/nikki-hiltz-trans-nonbinary-runner-now-awards-2023.

Hiltz, Nikki. “How Running and a Canceled Race Season Helped Me Come out as Trans, Nonbinary.” *Runner's World*, April 30, 2021, runnersworld.com/runners-stories/a36290808/nikki-hiltz-on-being-transgender-non-binary/.

Hiltz, Nikki. “Nikki Hiltz Blog #2.” *MileSplit CA*, Feb. 8, 2014, ca.milesplit.com/articles/120746/nikki-hiltz-blog-2.

*Instagram account: @nikkihiltz, instagram.com/nikkihiltz/.

Minsberg, Talya. “How Transgender Runner Nikki Hiltz Rose to the Top of Track.” *New York Times*, Aug. 19, 2023, nytimes.com/2023/08/19/sports/nikki-hiltz-world-championships.html.

*NBC Sports: “Nikki Hiltz breaks Meet Record in 1500m at Trials; punches ticket to Paris,” youtube.com/watch?v=k3aRTiNiR_w.

Monti, David. “Unstoppable Kipyegon Wins Fourth World 1500m Title.” Sept. 16, 2025. *Race Results Weekly*, runnerspace.com/gprofile.php?mgroup_id=44531&do=news&news_id=672944.

CHAPTER 10

CHELSEA GRAY, BASKETBALL "STARTS WITH INTEGRITY"

Personal interviews:
Chelsea Gray
Javon Gray
Vickey and James Gray
Tipesa Gray
Sean Watkins
Becky Hammon
George Quintero

Barnes. Katie. “How the Revival of Chelsea Gray Raises the Las Vegas Aces.” *ESPN*, Sept. 23, 2024, espn.com/wnba/story/_/id/41362282/2024-wnba-playoffs-chelsea-gray-invigorates-las-vegas-aces.

*Dapper, Michelle. "Stockton's Gray has High School Jersey Retired in Ceremony." *KCRA-TV*, Jan. 17, 2022, kcra.com/article/stocktons-chelsea-gray-high-school-jersey-retired-ceremony/38796871.

*Fin, Callie. "'Point Gawd' looks like herself during Aces 8-game winning streak." *Las Vegas Review-Journal*, Aug. 20, 2025, reviewjournal.com/sports/aces/point-gawd-looks-like-herself-during-aces-8-game-winning-streak-3427598/.

Laase, Eden. "How Chelsea Gray the Passer Became the WNBA's Point Gawd." *Just Women's Sports*, Aug. 26, 2022, justwomenssports.com/reads/chelsea-gray-las-vegas-aces-passing-wnba-playoffs/.

Thompson II, Marcus. "Chelsea Gray's Growth as a Baller and Activist is Also a Love Story." *The Athletic*, Sept. 17, 2020, nytimes.com/athletic/2073390/2020/09/17/thompson-chelsea-grays-growth-as-a-baller-and-activist-is-also-a-love-story/.

CHAPTER 11

NAOMI OSAKA, TENNIS "KNOW YOUR HISTORY"

Personal interviews:
Naomi Osaka
Zina Garrison
Kimiko Date

Badenhausen, Kurt. "Naomi Osaka is the Highest Paid Female Athlete Ever, Topping Serena Williams." *Forbes*, May 28, 2020, forbes.com/sites/kurtbadenhausen/2020/05/22/naomi-osaka-is-the-highest-paid-female-athlete-ever-topping-serena-williams/.

———. "Naomi Osaka's Historic Year Includes $55 Million Payday." *Sportico*, May 25, 2021, sportico.com/personalities/athletes/2021/naomi-osaka-2021-earnings-record-55-million-tennis-ace-1234630530/.

Clarey, Christopher. "At the French Open, Naomi Osaka Seeks Comfort in the Clay and No Interviews." *New York Times*, May 28, 2021, nytimes.com/2021/05/28/sports/tennis/french-open-2021-naomi-osaka.html.

*Futterman, Matthew. "Naomi Osaka Returns After Protest Prompts Tournament's Pause." *New York Times*, Aug. 28, 2020, nytimes.com/2020/08/28/sports/tennis/naomi-osaka.html.

Hernon, Matthew. "Kimiko Date: Celebrated Former Tennis Player Talks Trials, Triumphs and Wimbledon." *Metropolis*, July 1, 2021, metropolisjapan.com/kimiko-date/.

Holterman, Callie. "Meet the Artist Who Bedazzled Naomi Osaka's Labubus." *New York Times*, Sept. 4, 2025, nytimes.com/2025/09/04/style/naomi-osaka-labubu-us-open.html.

Hyde, David. "An uncommon dream came true on South Florida courts for Naomi Osaka." *South Florida Sun-Sentinel*, April 6, 2019, sun-sentinel.com/2019/03/16/an-uncommon-dream-came-true-on-south-florida-courts-for-naomi-osaka/.

King, Billie Jean. Foreword to *I Always Wanted to Be Somebody*. By Althea Gibson. New Chapter Press, 2021. Originally published in 1960.

Krueger, Alyson. "Naomi Osaka on Tennis and Childhood: 'Home Is Queens and These Courts.'" *New York Times*, Sept. 1, 2021, nytimes.com/2021/09/01/nyregion/naomi-osaka-jamaica-queens.html.

Larmer, Brook. "Naomi Osaka's Breakthrough Game." *New York Times Magazine*, Aug. 23, 2018, nytimes.com/2018/08/23/magazine/naomi-osakas-breakthrough-game.html.

Naomi Osaka: Netflix. Sports documentary, 2021.

Naomi Osaka: The Second Set. Tubi. Sports documentary, 2025.

"Naomi Osaka Tennis Biography." YouTube, 2013, youtube.com/watch?v=2v4f4nnJQmQ&embeds_referring_euri=https%3A%2F%2Fwww.si.com%2Ftennis%2F214%2F07%2F31%2Fwatch-naomi-osaka-bank-west-classic-forehand-highlight&source_ve_path=OTY3MTQ.

Nguyen, Courtney. "Watch: 16-year-old standout Naomi Osaka hits a massive forehand." *Sports Illustrated*, July 31, 2014, si.com/tennis/2014/07/31/watch-naomi-osaka-bank-west-classic-forehand-highlight.

*Osaka, Naomi. "I Never Would've Imagined Writing This Two Years Ago." *Esquire Magazine*, July 1, 2020, esquire.com/sports/a33022329/naomi-osaka-op-ed-george-floyd-protests/.

*Osaka, Naomi. "It's O.K. Not to Be O.K." *Time* magazine, July 8, 2021, time.com/6077128/naomi-osaka-essay-tokyo-olympics/.

Rothenberg, Ben. *Naomi Osaka: Her Journey to Finding Her Power and Her Voice.* New York: Dutton, 2024.

*Naomi Yamaguchi. "Ōsaka Tamaki: Mom of Tennis Star Ōsaka Naomi on Life and Her Daughter's Determination." *Nippon.com*, July 12, 2022, nippon.com/en/japan-topics/g02138/.

*US Open Championships, 2025. Naomi Osaka Press Conferences, YouTube.

Yomiuri Shimbun. "Raising Naomi, as Told by Her Mother / Naomi Osaka's Mother Sustained Family on 3 Hrs of Sleep." Aug. 11, 2023, japannews.yomiuri.co.jp/society/social-series/20230811-129117/.

*Yoshikawa, Mai, "Naomi Osaka on tennis, motherhood and being Japanese," *Japan Times*, Feb. 26, 2025, metropolisjapan.com/kimiko-date/.

PICTURE CREDITS

Introduction
New York Historical: 11

Chapter 1: Caitlin Clark, Basketball
Dickson Jensen / All Iowa Attack: 14; University of Iowa, Brian Ray / Stephen Mally: 28-29; Getty Images: Dylan Goodman: 34, Justin Casterline: 37.

Chapter 2: Diana Flores, Flag Football
Diana Flores: 40, 44; Xinhua / Alamy: 57, 58.

Chapter 3: Kendall Coyne Schofield, Ice Hockey
Kendall Coyne Schofield: 60, 66, 70; Bill Smith / Getty Images: 77; Professional Women's Hockey League: 79, 81.

Chapter 4: Midge Purce, Soccer
Gotham FC: 84, 101, 104; Midge Purce: 88, 92.

Chapter 5: Asjia O'Neal, Volleyball
Jeffrey McWhorter: 106; Mesha O'Neal: 120; Texas Athletics: 123, 124; LOVB: 127.

Chapter 6: Kelsie Whitmore, Baseball
Richard Hopkins: 128; Scott Whitmore: 131, 133; The Savannah Bananas / Amelia Berg: 146; Jackie Kalafut: 148.

Chapter 7: Amit Elor, Wrestling
Tony Rotundo / WrestlersAre Warriors.com: 150, 165; Amit Elor: 156, 162; Elizabeth Fox: 168.

Chapter 8: McKenzie Coan, Swimming
U.S. Olympic & Paralympic Committee: 171,190; McKenzie Coan: 177, 185, 188.

Chapter 9: Nikki Hiltz, Track
Kevin Morris: 194, 215; Hiltz family: 199; Shmuel Thaler: 202; Nikki Hiltz: 208.

Chapter 10: Chelsea Gray, Basketball
Duke Athletics: 218; Chelsea Gray: 222; Saint Mary's High School / Vladimir Kozina: 227; Getty Images: David Becker: 235, Gregory Shamus: 237.

Chapter 11: Naomi Osaka, Tennis
Getty Images: Clive Brunskill: 242, Ezra Shaw: 249, Robert Prange: 265; AP Images: Frank Franklin II: 257 (top two), Seth Wenig: 257 (bottom two); ZUMA Press, Inc. / Alamy: 260.